Father
Fiction

—■—

Other books by Donald Miller

Through Painted Deserts
Blue Like Jazz
Searching for God Knows What
A Million Miles in a Thousand Years

Father Fiction

Chapters for a Fatherless Generation

Donald Miller

Previously published as
To Own a Dragon

HOWARD BOOKS
A DIVISION OF SIMON & SCHUSTER, INC.

New York · Nashville · London · Toronto · Sydney

Howard Books
A Division of Simon & Schuster, Inc.
1230 Avenue of the Americas, New York, NY 10020

In association with the literary agency of Creative Trust, Inc.

Certain names and identifying characteristics have been changed.

First Howard Books trade paperback edition February 2011

HOWARD and colophon are registered trademarks of Simon & Schuster, Inc.

Previously published as *To Own a Dragon*.

For information regarding special discounts for bulk purchases, please contact Simon & Schuster Special Sales at 1-866-506-1949 or business@simonandschuster.com.

The Simon & Schuster Speakers Bureau can bring authors to your live event. For more information or to book an event, contact the Simon & Schuster Speakers Bureau at 1-866-248-3049 or visit our website at www.simonspeakers.com.

Edited by Philis Boultinghouse

Designed by Level C, Inc.

Manufactured in the United States of America

10 9 8 7 6 5 4 3 2 1

The Library of Congress has cataloged the hardcover edition as follows:
Miller, Donald, 1971–
    Father fiction : chapters for a fatherless generation / Donald Miller.—
[Rev. ed.].
      p. cm.
    Rev. ed. of: To own a dragon. c2006.
    1. Fatherhood—Religious aspects—Christianity. 2. Miller, Donald,
1971– I. Miller, Donald, 1971– To own a dragon. II. Title.
    BV4529.17.M55   2010
    248.8'421—dc22   2009044014

ISBN 978-1-4391-6916-2
ISBN 978-1-4391-9053-1 (pbk)
ISBN 978-1-4391-6919-3 (ebook)

Scripture quotations are taken from the King James version.

For the staff, the interns, and especially the mentors at
The Mentoring Project

Contents

Introduction

Rewriting the Story of Fatherlessness

I used to hate talking about father issues. It made me feel weak, honestly. I felt like a sickly kid, complaining about life. And I loathe self-pity in almost any form. That's why I hated writing this book. I went up to my friend's cabin on Orcas Island and holed up, *me and my father issues*. Lots of crying, lots of deleting everything I'd written the night before. And the whole time I was feeling like half a man.

It took about a year to write this little book, and another couple months in that cabin to edit it and get it right. It's the hardest book I've ever written, I think, not because it was a literary challenge but because it was an emotional challenge. I kept having to go places I didn't want to go, to think about things I didn't want to think about. I'd wake up and get emotionally emasculated every day, complaining about how

Dad wasn't around when I was a kid. Part of me wanted to admit it hurt, and the other part of me was too numb to care. He left, so what? I didn't need him. I made it without him.

I'm thirty-eight years old, and I still need a father. Right now I'm sitting in the back of a tour bus, on a sixty-five-city book tour where lots of people come out to hear whatever my new book is about. But in so many ways I'm still that kid, not sure exactly how to be emotionally intimate with a girl without feeling weak, not sure my work is good enough, not sure if the people who are clapping would really like me if they got to know me. I attribute a lot of those insecurities to father issues. And any confidence I have I attribute to having worked through father issues. Everybody is insecure, and not everybody who grew up without a father lacks confidence and emotional health, but the connection between the two is undeniable.

I released this book with a small publisher a few years ago, and even though it hardly got placement in bookstores, it sold a lot of copies. Everywhere I went people would come up and say this book affected them more than any other. I wanted to take them aside as though they'd read some truly secret journal I'd written. I wanted to pull them into the alley behind the venue and say, "Look, man, if you tell anybody else I struggle . . ." Not sure what I'd do. I'm not much of a fighter. But I was ashamed of the crap I had to work through in order to feel like a man.

Things are changing, though, and men are beginning to talk about their issues. We are moving the conversation out of the alleys and into public forums. Improvement has been made in the talkability of fatherhood issues. Tim Russert wrote about it from a positive perspective, writing that wonderful book about his father. And President Barack Obama talked about it from a position of strength, openly discussing his hardship as a young, fatherless man and the mentors and figures that helped him overcome.

Even though this book is about fatherlessness, it's certainly not only for men. Women suffer from father issues, too, obviously. They may suffer more. I believe something magical happens when a father tells his daughter she is beautiful, that she is a woman, and that she has a reason to be respected and loved by a good man. If she doesn't get this message from her dad, she will look for it from men who have less pure motives. Women tend to become victims when they grow up without good fathers. Men tend to become oppressors. I heard recently that 94 percent of people in prison are men. And 85 percent of those men grew up in fatherless homes.

If we have a crisis in this country, it's more than a fatherless crisis, though. It's a crisis of manhood, of masculinity. It's affecting our families, our schools, it's filling our prisons, and it's killing the hearts of our women.

I've started a mentoring program that offers resources to the 360,000 churches in America, to provide mentors for the 27 million kids growing up without fathers. I am convinced that within twenty years, we can shut down prisons because we have provided positive male role models for kids who would otherwise be headed for trouble. I am convinced we can curb teen suicide, unwanted pregnancy and abortion, and turn back the tidal divorce rate if we step in and provide mentors for kids without dads.

That said, this book is not about a movement that is happening, because a movement isn't happening. The statistics are getting worse. This book is about the hard, shameful, embarrassing stuff you and I have to work through as an individual. It's about me secretly admitting to you I needed a father, and how I felt like half a man until I dealt with those issues honestly. And if you let it, this book is an informal guide to pulling the rotted beams out of from your foundation and replacing them with something you can build a life on.

It's time to rewrite the story of fatherlessness in America. It's time to start a movement in which we openly and honestly address our weaknesses so we can find strength. My hope is that Fathers won't be Fiction much longer. The movement starts with you.

Best,
Donald Miller

1

The Replacements

We've Got Men on the Ground

In the absence of a real father, I had a cast of characters that were at times hilarious, pitiful, perfect, kind, and wise.

Here they are. . . .

My first father was a black man on television who wore bright argyle sweaters. He lived in New York or Chicago, I can't remember which. He was incredibly intelligent and had a knockout wife. I'm talking about Bill Cosby. When I was a kid, I wanted to be Theo Huxtable. I liked the way Theo dressed. I liked that he was confident with women and even though he didn't make good grades, he still felt good about himself. Plus, he had good-looking sisters—one older, two younger—who always gave him encouragement and advice about life, along with safe male–female tension. I liked that Bill Cosby had money, too, tons of cash and certain philosophies about saving and spending that gave the family a sense of security, that turned his knockout wife on and had her singing slow, sultry blues melodies to him from the bed while he brushed his teeth in the master bathroom. Bill Cosby never panicked about small things, he never got worked up about broken windows or cereal on the floor, and if he did get worked up, it was more like a comedy routine than a drunken rampage. He also laughed at himself, which was endearing, and I would sit in front of the little television in my room and live vicariously through the made-up life of the Huxtables, who had celebrity guests coming through the house every few episodes to play the trombone or tapdance.

My mom was great, don't get me wrong, but the only guests we ever had at our house were from the singles group at church, and none of them ever whipped out a trombone to play "When the Saints Go Marching In" or tapdanced in the living room or recited a piece of epic prose about the underground railroad in which "our people" traversed from oppression and slavery to freedom. Our guests, rather, ate meatballs on paper plates and talked bitterly about their ex-husbands.

I also liked the fact that, on *The Cosby Show*, there was never any serious conflict. When Theo graduated from college, for example, the conflict simply involved the family only having ten tickets to the graduation ceremony. Bill wanted to invite the whole neighborhood. All the ladies kept looking at him and shaking their heads because Bill Cosby's love for his family was always causing him to make a mess of things. They would shake their heads and laugh, and he would make a funny face, and Theo would throw his hands up, look at the ceiling, and roll his eyes while exclaiming, "*Gosh, Dad!*" and I would roll over backwards on the floor and look up at the ceiling, sigh, and say under my breath, *Black people have it perfect.*

White people had interesting fathers, too, but nothing to make a sitcom about. When I was growing up my friend Tom had a father, and I learned from him that a real father doesn't have jazz singers over to perform in the living room before dinner, and that real families with fathers don't lip-sync Motown tunes or give speeches at college graduations. Rather, real fathers, at least at Tom's house, clean guns while watching television, weed-eat the lawn with one hand while holding a beer in the other, and squeeze their wife's butt in the kitchen while she's cooking dinner. And because of Tom's father and because I watched *The Cosby Show* with the devotion of a Muslim, I came to believe a man was supposed to be around the house to arm and disarm weapons, make sexual advances on the matriarch, perform long and colorful ad-libs with children about why they should clean their room, and above all, always face the camera, even if the entire family has to sit on one side of the table during dinner.

MY MOTHER WAS the only female father in my Cub Scout troop, and God knows she tried. But the truth is she had no idea what she was doing. We had a pinewood derby car race where you had to carve a car out of a block of wood, then set it on a ramp and race some other guy with a pinewood car. I came in dead last. The night we made the cars my mom dropped me off at the den mother's house and trusted the fathers who were in the garage making their sons' cars to also help make mine. They didn't. I didn't care. I just wanted to drill holes in the cement driveway with a cordless drill. I don't even think my car had wheels when it came time to race, just a lot of WD-40 on the bottom of a block of wood and a stripe down the side like that car in *The Dukes of Hazzard*.

On race night, with a hundred Boy Scouts standing around and two hundred moms and dads standing around with them, my block of wood slid down the ramp at quarter-speed and came to a sudden stop right about the time the ramp gave way to flatness. Everybody got quiet. I just stood there with my hands on my hips, shaking my head saying, "That General Lee, always breaking down!" My mom was terribly upset about the incident, but I didn't realize it at the time. We picked up the General Lee and left early, right after my mother had sharp words for the men in our den group, who spoke sharply back to her about a driveway full of drill holes.

Mom kept trying. She asked our landlord's son, who was a pothead, if he would take me to the Boy Scout father-and-son campout. His name was Matt, and he drove a yellow Volkswagen bug and listened to Lynyrd Skynyrd tapes and ended every sentence with the phrase "Do you know what I mean, dude?" He was pretty cool, but I think he felt out of place around the other fathers, men who were approximately twenty years older than he was and drove trucks or minivans and were married and rarely, if ever, smoked pot, or, for that matter, listened to Lynyrd Skynyrd.

I think both of us felt out of place at the father-and-son campout. After all, we had only met once before, when Matt had come over to the house to change the lightbulbs on the front and back porch.

"Hey, little man," he said to me, looking down from his ladder, *"how can I put a bulb in this thing when there's already a bulb in it? Do you know what I mean, dude?"*

On the last night of the campout, we were sitting around a fire and the fathers were telling about their favorite memory with their sons, and when it came time for Matt to talk about me, he sat silent for a minute. As I said, Matt and I had spent little time together before the campout. I was searching my mind for any kind of memory, and considered talking about that great time he changed the light bulbs, how he had to move the ladder a couple times, and how I helped him by turning the switch on and off. I knew it was a boring story, but I thought I might embellish it a bit by insisting that both of us got electrocuted and had to give each other CPR. But then Matt broke the silence. Having searched for any kind of memory himself, he told about the car ride on the way *to* the campout: how we stopped at McDonald's and had to jump-start the bug and how we played air guitar and bashed our heads against the dashboard to the tune of "Sweet Home Alabama."

"Times with our sons or with our neighbors' kids are important, do you know what I mean, dude?" Matt said to the fathers, most of them looking very confused. I nodded my head.

"I know what you mean," I said, breaking the awkward silence.

"Sure you do, Doug," he chortled, rubbing my head.

"Don," I corrected. "My name is Don."

"Sure it is, little man," he said to me with a confused look on his face.

Then Matt, realizing his story had fallen flat, started telling us how he made out with a cheerleader in the janitor's closet when he was in high school. Another father stopped him just short of second base. A prepubescent, collective grunt went out when the story was interrupted, but Matt finished it the next day when we were waiting in line to get in a canoe. The smell of ammonia, apparently, still turned him on.

———■———

MATT WAS GREAT, but not much of a guide in the father sense. And he went off to the army shortly after the campout, so I never learned important things he knew like how to actually *get* the girl to go *into* the janitor's closet or how to drive for two years without a license.

The next guy was more fatherly but straight as an arrow, which was nice for a change, but he was also nuts. His name was Mr. Kilpin, and he went to our church. His thing was to fly remote control airplanes in a field. It was exciting at first, for about twenty minutes or so, but he would never let me control the plane. He would stand there wearing some sort of military hat he must have picked up in Vietnam, and his eyes would get big as planets as he made the plane dip down and sweep across the field, all the while making bombing noises with his mouth.

"Did you see that, Donald?" he'd ask.

"You got those commie bastards," I'd say, sort of looking around for a Frisbee or something. I kept asking, every two minutes, if he would let me fly the plane, but each time he would say maybe next time, maybe just for a few seconds the next time we went out. I had to endure three weekends of simulated bombing runs over the Mekong Delta before he finally gave in to my pestering and let me take the sticks. Within eight seconds I had flown the thing into a tree, at which point Mr. Kilpin shrieked and ran across the field, shouting "We've got men down, we've got men on the ground!"

All the way home he lectured me about the kinds of torture a captured pilot has to endure, and we never spent any time together after that.

THE NEXT GUY was an enormous improvement and proved to be just what I needed as a makeshift father figure. He was the youth minister at my church and was hired about the time I started junior high. His name was David Gentiles, and because most last names are derived from what our ancestors did for a living, I assumed David had come from a small community that politely wanted to differentiate itself from Jews. David could never authenticate my suspicion, but I told him this was probably the case. I lived about three blocks from the church, so I would go over and visit David in his office. I sat across from him, talking about the state of affairs in the world, football, the weather, girls, all the while going through his desk looking for rubber bands I could shoot at him while he tried to study the Bible. I'd find pencils I could fling into the ceiling tiles, or I'd explain, at length, the many ways he could rearrange his office. David never asked me to leave, and looking back I have no idea why. Either he enjoyed being around me, or he was a good actor. Regardless, he liked my ideas and would nod in agreement when I told him he didn't need a desk, that Ronald Reagan worked standing up, and this would free space in his office for a small putting green and a contraption that shoots the golf ball back to you.

I used to sit and look at the books on David's shelf, asking intelligent and probing questions about each one.

"What's that book about the Civil War about?" I'd say.

"The Civil War," he'd answer.

"What about that one about Abraham Lincoln?"

"That one's just a cookbook," he'd tell me.

After I inquired about twenty or so of his books, he asked if I was interested in books. I told him I didn't know anything about them, that the problem with most books is they were too long. Then he turned me on to some poetry, which was good because it was shorter. David said girls just loved the stuff. I went home and read through a lot of it and memorized a couple, and he seemed pretty impressed with that. He asked me, a little later, if I had ever thought about writing. He told me he thought I had a knack for understanding poetry and wondered if I would be interested in writing a guest editorial for the youth group newsletter.

"I've seen a lot of growth in you, Don," he said while we were walking down the church hallway. "You've really got a way with words, and your spiritual life has developed uniquely, quite beautifully, and I feel like you could deal with spirituality in a delicate manner, getting to the heart of our faith. Would you be interested in writing an article?"

"Does the pope crap in the woods?" I told him.

I spent the next week poring over the dictionary for the biggest, most obscure words I could find—words like *loquacious* and *flabbergasted.* I was going to knock Dave's socks off with my smarts. The first sentence of my article read: "The loquaciousness of pious rhetoric has developed into a pariah in the corridors of First Baptist Church."

The article was about how everybody was stupid except for me and Dave, and went on to name the top ten most boring people at First Baptist Church.

I turned the article in to David, and he sat behind his desk and kind of hummed and coughed as he read, his eyes getting big and his hands flattening the paper and his head suddenly jolting back when he came to the end of a paragraph. He put his hand on his forehead and looked at me in bewilderment, probably wondering how such brilliant writing could come at such a young age. "Good use of exclamation points," he finally said. "Your punctuation is remarkable."

And looking back, I believe it was. I've always been good at punctuation!

David kindly explained, however, the article might be a bit critical, and I might consider writing about something I like—people I like, perhaps—or do a review of a movie or a record, or maybe write up a concert or something going on at school. I told him those were all good ideas, but as a journalist, I would need to make up my own mind about what I would write and that, as much as I respected him, I wasn't going to be a pawn of The Man.

"Would never ask you to compromise," David said.

"Thanks," I told him, leaning back in my chair and crossing my legs. "I'm not a fan of corporate."

"Me neither," he said with a confused look on his face.

There happened to be a talent show going on at school that week, and I decided I would interview some of the talent and write a review. I sat in the back with a notebook on my lap, hoping people would ask why I had that notebook on my lap, or for that matter a pencil behind each ear, or for that matter a hat with an index card on which was printed the word *PRESS*. I roamed during the show, walking the aisles, trying to get a feel for audience reaction. Then I went backstage as a band called Dead Man Sweat did a partially intelligible, twelve-minute rendition of "Pour Some Sugar on Me," toward the end of which the lead singer opened a bag of sugar and poured it over his long, dark hair, causing the principal to put an end to the music. The lead singer had to sweep up the mess before three girls came out and did a dance from the movie *Flashdance*. The girls danced sultrily against and on top of chairs as some guys from the football team squirted water on them from the wings. This was also, unfortunately, interrupted. But I interviewed them all. I interviewed the rock band, asking: "Sugar is a metaphor for what?" Earlier that week, I had learned what a metaphor was, and the concept fascinated me. "Leg warmers are a metaphor for what?" I asked the girls who did the *Flashdance*.

Then this girl came up, this girl from my youth group, whom I had mostly ignored that year, and she stepped to the microphone and shyly said, "Hello," and that she would like to sing a Christian song for Jesus. I dropped my pencil. It's social suicide, I thought. You can't sing a song for Jesus at a high school talent show. The audience threw out some cold remarks about going back to Mayberry, and when the piano accompaniment started, she belted out quite possibly the worst rendition of "His Eye Is on the Sparrow" ever performed, save Roger Bobo's tuba rendition with the Canadian Brass.

The crowd had a field day. It was like *The Gong Show*. People were rolling in the aisles. And standing backstage I started feeling a little sorry for her, and then something strange happened in my chest. What I mean is, there is this fight or flight thing that happens when you decide whether you are going to associate with—or disassociate yourself from—somebody who has farted in public or coughed up their food, whether you were going to say you never knew her, didn't attend the same church, or whether you were going to, well, clap. And I clapped. I mean when she finished, I clapped, and I meant it. It felt good to take a stand for somebody who nobody else was taking a stand for. And she came off the stage and I asked her what the sparrow was a metaphor for, and then I told her I thought she did a great job, that I was proud of her. She looked at me with this huge smile, and you could tell she was very nervous and relieved at the same time. And I went home that night and wrote an article saying I thought God might have been kind of happy with the talent show, and I wrote about how I thought we should all be willing to make complete idiots of ourselves for God, and how even if our voices sounded like *a chicken in a cage with a ferret*, we should be willing to praise God with the pipes God gave us. The tag line at the end of the article, the real clincher, the tearjerker exclamation point, was this:

And even though everybody in the auditorium was booing that night, and even though Monica shouldn't be allowed to sing the national anthem at a chess tournament, the angels in heaven were clapping, and the opinions of angels matter more than the opinions of men, because angels can fly.

I gave the article to Monica first, and I stood there while she read it, and about halfway through her eyes started to water, and about three-fourths through she put her hand over her mouth, and when she finished she looked me in the eye with the most tender, vulnerable look, dropped the piece of paper and ran down the hall of the math wing. I knew then that I had the gift—that David Gentiles was right, that I could move people with words, encourage them and change their lives forever. And even though Dave thought it best I rewrite the article and take out several of the harsher adjectives and the bit about the *chicken in the cage with the ferret*, the thing still had power. I got a lot of calls from people at the church, and people stopped me in the halls to say "*good job,*" and "*that line about angels having wings was an interesting point.*"

I only tell you this to say David Gentiles, who could have done just about anything else with his time, decided to spend time with me and give me a shot at writing. He was somebody who stepped into my life and helped me believe I was here on purpose and for a purpose. I don't think there are very many things more important than this when we are kids.

The truth I've learned about life is you can't do it on your own. People don't do well independently. One generation passes wisdom to the next, wisdom about girls and faith and punctuation. And you won't be as good a person if you don't receive it.

And in life, I figure, you are going to pretty much do the things that make you feel good about yourself, make you feel important and on purpose, and walk away from the things that make you feel like a loser. I distinctly remember this phase in my life, this time when I started writing, as a kind of fork in the road. On one hand, a good friend and I had just discovered a quick and easy way to break into houses, stealing loose change from jars on people's dressers. And then there was this writing thing going on, and it wasn't like I was deciding which person I was going to become; it's more like I was swimming in a river and there were two equal currents. I could have very easily ended up in prison—first breaking into houses, then falling in with the wrong crowd, then drugs, and so on and so on. A statistic. David Gentiles was the person who threw out a rope. He was a father figure. People assume when you're swimming in a river you are supposed to know which way you are going, and I guess some of the time that is true, but there are certain currents that are very strong, and it's when we are in those currents we need somebody to come along, pull us out, and guide us in a safer direction.

2

Our Problem

To Own a Dragon

All my life I have been fascinated by stuff that isn't there.

I'd be lying if I said I read books early. I didn't start reading till I was in college, but I knew about fairies and dragons and trolls from hearing about them at reading time when the librarian at my elementary school crossed her long legs and sat silently until we sat silently. Then she'd wrap her lips around the simple words of a children's book, holding her palm against the crease of the page, turning the book toward us to display the watercolor pictures—a small troll in a big coat who lived under a bridge, his eye ever-alert for travelers on the road. I remember a book with pictures of a boy riding a dragon through the clouds, smoke and fire coming from the creature's nostrils, the boy leaning in as the dragon ascended over a pleasant village. And I remember wondering what it would be like to own a dragon, to lie across the monster's spine, inching toward its neck as the beast jolted into flight, thrusting through the milky pretext for heaven that glows over Houston, up and above the weather where my dragon and I could watch lightning fight itself into exhaustion.

I bring this up because in writing some thoughts about a father, or not having a father, I feel as though I'm writing a book about a troll under a bridge or a dragon. For me, a father was nothing more than a character in a fairy tale. I know fathers are not like dragons because fathers actually exist. I have seen them on television and sliding their arms around their wives in grocery stores, and I have seen them in the malls and in the coffee shops, but these were characters in other people's stories. The sad thing is, as a kid, I wondered why I couldn't have a dragon, but I never wondered why I didn't have a father.

I don't say this out of self-pity, because I didn't miss having a father. But as I grew older, I found myself wondering if I had missed out on something important.

What I mean is that by design, within the laws of nature, a man and a woman join and make kids. It's the natural order of things. And the natural order of things means something. There aren't a lot of things on this planet that aren't connected to other things, interdependent, making everything work out like they're supposed to. And at least you'd assume the father is supposed to stick around and teach his kids to carve a turkey at Thanksgiving or whatever it is a father teaches a kid. But that never happened to me, and if you're reading this book, it may have never happened to you either.

It makes you wonder if by having a dad around—just his being there reading the morning paper and smoking cigars at poker with his friends and having him read you a story at night—you were supposed to understand something. Lately, I have been curious about what that something is, and whether or not a person could understand it even if his father took off.

———————————————

I LEARNED A great deal about myself while watching a documentary a few years ago about elephants in a wildlife trust in Africa. There were twenty-five elephants, all of them orphans, and they had been brought to the trust twenty years before. They were becoming teenagers—in elephant years. The girls were adequate, getting along with the other elephants, but there were a few boys who were causing a great deal of trouble. The narrator talked about the frustrations these few elephants were feeling because they had gone into early musth cycles, which showed up as a green pus running down their right hind leg. This phase produced aggressive and violent behavior, the elephant equivalent of sexual frustration.

The narrator in the documentary said the elephant musth

cycle begins in adolescence and normally lasts only a few days. But among these orphans, the musth cycle was disrupted and had become unusually long. These elephants were taking out their aggression on rhinos that bathed at a local mud pool. An elephant would slowly lumber down to the pool, enter near a rhino, then spear it through the side with his tusks. Then the elephant would lean his gargantuan forehead into the head of the rhino, holding the beast underwater until it drowned. The filmmakers followed these orphan elephants, who were always on their own, staggering about the wildlife refuge, fueled by a pent-up aggression they couldn't understand. They weren't acting like elephants—they didn't know what an elephant was supposed to do with all his energy, all his muscle.

Occasionally, two elephants in musth would meet, and the encounter was always violent, going so far as to uproot trees in the fray of the brawl. When both beasts, bloodied, lumbered their separate ways alone—without a family, without a tribe—I couldn't help but identify. I have never killed a rhino, or much of anything for that matter, but there have been times in my life when I didn't know exactly how to be. I mean, there were feelings, sometimes anger, sometimes depression, sometimes raging lust, and I was never sure what any of it was about. I just felt like killing somebody or sleeping with some girl or decking a guy in a bar, and I didn't know what to do with any of these feelings. Life was a confusing series of emotions rubbing against events. I wasn't sure how to manage myself, how to talk to a woman, how to build a career, how to—well, be a man.

To me, life was something you had to stumble through alone. It wasn't something you enjoyed or conquered, it was something that happened to you, and you didn't have a whole lot of say about the way it turned out. You just acted out your feelings and hoped you'd never get caught.

On television that night, however, the narrator began to speak of a kind of hope for these elephants. Elephant development, apparently, begins very early. Female elephants are only capable of having children once every two years, and during those two years between babies, the young are obsessively cared for by their mothers. They are fed, sheltered, loved, and guided in their learning of basic survival.

It is only at the first musth cycle that a young male elephant leaves his mother and enters into the African wild, searching for a mentor, a guide. The green pus running down his hind leg and his smell like fresh-cut grass alerts an older, fully mature male, that this is a young elephant in need of guidance. Upon finding a mentor, the young elephant's musth cycle ends. The older and younger begin to travel together, to find food together, to protect each other—the older one teaching the younger what elephant strength is for and how to use it for the benefit of himself and the tribe.

Watching television that night, I wondered if humans aren't like that too. I began to wonder if we guys weren't designed to have a father whose very presence would cause us to understand more accurately what our muscle is for, what we are supposed to do with our energy.

You have to wonder, don't you? Some statistics state as many as 85 percent of people in prison grew up without a dad.

And so watching the documentary, I began to wonder if those of us without dads aren't making mistakes in our lives we wouldn't make if we had a father to guide us. I wondered if people who grow up with great fathers don't walk around with a subconscious sense they are wanted on this planet, that they belong, and the world needs them. And I wondered this: Is there practical information we are supposed to know about work, relationships, decisions, authority, leadership, marriage, and family that we would have learned if there were a guide around to help us navigate our journey? I wondered if some of the confusing emotions I was feeling weren't a kind of suspended adolescence from which the presence of an older man might have delivered me.

3

The Mentor

Terri Said I Could Make a Sandwich

I thought the confusion I felt growing up without a father was just part of life, and there seemed to be benefits. Without the authoritarian structure of two parents, I could get away with a great deal more. And I disliked authority figures, because they represented boundaries. The worst authority figures were older men. For reasons I didn't understand when I was younger, I resented them. I felt as though they wanted me to submit to their authority because they wanted to feel powerful. But I also wanted their respect and approval. And if I sensed disapproval, I belittled them in my mind. I was a split person: Half of me wanted to be mentored through life—the side, I suppose, that wanted a father—and the other half would rather not answer to anybody. I started realizing this several years ago when I moved in with a family, the family of a man who taught a college class at a church I was attending.

I met John MacMurray at a strange time in my life. I had left my home in Houston and was traveling around the country when I ran out of money in Oregon. I got an apartment in the suburbs of Portland where housing was cheap, and I started going to a church in a town called Boring, Oregon. The town lived up to its name. It had one stoplight, a convenience store, and a burger place. It was very beautiful, mind you, with views of Mount Hood and Mount St. Helens, river valleys and all, but once you were over that stuff, there wasn't much going on. The church I started attending was in the middle of a shrub farm—landscape shrubs and flowers and Christmas trees. Every November, the Christmas trees would be hauled down to people in Florida who paid fifty bucks to hang lights on them, sing some songs, then watch them dry up and get pine tar all over the wicker furniture. This church was crowded with tree farmers, hunters, fishermen, that sort of thing—men's men.

I was born going to church, raised going to church, and church had been a significant part of my life. I confess it's been comforting to me, at dark times, to know there is a God in the cosmos who is paying attention. I had walked away from a lot of it, but when I moved to Oregon, I was feeling lonely so I decided to plug back in to a church. They had a college group that met at a guy's house way out in the sticks, this guy I was telling you about, and I started driving out there once a week.

At first, I didn't know what to think of the group. Or of John MacMurray, the guy who led it. We would sit around in his big living room, on the floor, because he and his wife didn't have very much furniture. After we made small talk for a while, John would sit down in a chair, the only chair in the room, and everybody would get quiet. This took me a while to get used to, and I don't mean to make the guy sound like a strange guru or something—it's just that when he sat down in the chair, everybody shut up, waiting for him to speak. And the first thing John would say was, "What do you guys want to talk about?" The hush made me wonder what kind of guy I was dealing with, and I half expected him to lay his Bible across his lap, press his palms together, nod slowly, and say something like: "In order for us to become great, we must make ourselves small"—and everybody would respond with a worshipful sigh, to which I would have laughed out loud. Thank heavens, nothing like this happened. He turned out to be pretty normal, and the hush that came over the group was mostly because people didn't want to miss anything.

I'd attend these meetings about once a week, fairly faithfully and began to make some friends in the group, including John. John can, at first, come off a bit cocky. It's not a bad cocky—in fact, it's quite endearing sometimes, once you get used to it. Partly, he has this personality trait because he grew up in Philadelphia, and roughly everybody from Philadelphia sounds like they think they are better than you. It's true. Panhandlers on the street sound condescending in Philadelphia. Anyway, we all grew to like it. Sometimes you get tired of people kissing your butt all the time, and you just wish someone would speak their mind. That's John.

For a living, John was a photographer. He didn't take pictures of people, he took pictures of landscapes, of mountains and rivers and this sort of thing. I found this out because some of us would stay around after the Bible study and watch whatever was on television, and one time I asked John about the photographs he and his wife had hanging in the living room. They had landscape photographs, meadows and snow and sunsets and the like, a couple of them on the walls and one of them over the fireplace. These weren't normal nature photographs, like the ones your uncle took of the family in front of a waterfall in Kentucky, but the real thing, almost like art. These were the sort of photographs you took by being dropped off by helicopter on a mountaintop just at sunrise, no footprints or anything. And that's when John told me they were his. I didn't believe him at first, but he shook his head and shrugged his shoulders like it didn't matter whether I believed him or not. That's when I started thinking maybe he was telling the truth.

We'd hang out after college group, sitting in the den watching *Sports Center*, and one evening John asked if I wanted to see some of his work. The rest of the guys got quiet. Sure, whatever, I said. The others stood up, and John looked at them with this kind of Bruce Willis glance and said, "I guess you guys want to see, too."

We went upstairs to John's office where there were stacks of black boxes all over the floor and on the desk, and John led us meandering through them. He flipped a switch on his desk and half the thing lit up—not a top light, but the actual desk was made of glass and it was lit from underneath. John opened one of the black boxes and set a couple slides on the backlit desk. These slides were pretty big, four inches by five, John told me, and when they were lit from behind they were remarkable. I couldn't believe a guy could get paid to go to the most beautiful places in the world to take pictures.

John would tell us what they were—one a mountaintop in Italy, the next the Great Barrier Reef in Australia, then a waterfall in the Jefferson Wilderness here in Oregon. He must have had more than a hundred slides in each box, and there were hundreds of boxes. All the guys stood around the light board like we were looking at pictures of naked ladies, because we were honestly amazed. None of us able to take it all in—the perfection of the colors and the textures, moonlight reflecting on a glacier with a gray mountain peak in silhouette rising up in the background, a single flower in a meadow along a creek banked with green moss, pines so thick with snow you could hardly see the green within the pure white pillows that piled along their laboring branches, water surging over a five-hundred-foot cliff to a blue pool below the water seeming to move in the still photo.

There were times we would meet at John's house and somebody else would substitute teach, and John would come back the next week with another stack of slides—fall colors on the Blue Ridge Parkway, winter in a Scottish glen, the Swiss Alps, ranges in New Zealand that you hardly believed were real. I asked him why he didn't put his name in huge letters at the bottom of his photos and make a fortune off posters at tourist shops in Yosemite Park or somewhere. But he rolled his eyes.

"I'm serious," I said. "You could get some serious cash out of this stuff."

"I do fine," John said.

"I'm just saying," I told him.

I got to feeling pretty comfortable around the MacMurrays. After a while, you don't notice that whole Philadelphia thing, and it hardly mattered because we were learning the Bible inside and out. I even started going over there when there wasn't a Bible study. Terri, John's wife, would invite me out for Saturday breakfast, and then we'd all sit and watch golf or talk about John's last trip. They had this little boy named Chris, who was cute as a puppy, and it didn't hurt that Terri looked like a supermodel either. John would make eyes at her while she chased Chris around the island in the kitchen. I liked being with them and was kind of honored that good-looking, rich people would want me hanging around.

One night after Bible study, I was feeling pretty hungry because I hadn't eaten any dinner. I went to the kitchen, and Terri said I could make myself a sandwich. I'm not the type to go rummaging around in somebody else's fridge without permission, but Terri said I could. And there I was all aglow in the light of the refrigerator when John walked into the kitchen.

"Well, make yourself at home, Miller," he said to me.

"Terri said I could make a sandwich."

"Let me know if I can make you a quiche or something," he said.

"Terri said I could make a sandwich."

"Well, you might as well move in if you're going to eat all our food," John said to me, smiling. "You can pick up the key from Terri. The apartment is above the garage." And with that, he walked back into the living room. I got a plate out of the cupboard and was opening a loaf of bread when Terri walked through the swinging door from the living room.

"It will be great to have another man around," she said. "I always have to lift those bags of pellets for the wood stove when John is out taking pictures, but you can do that. I'll get you a key."

"A key to what?" I asked.

"The apartment is above the garage," she said, and pulled a key out of the junk drawer. "You should just do what John tells you. It's easier that way," she said, handing me the key.

"You guys really want me to move in?" I asked.

"Guess so," she said with a smile.

So that is how I moved in with John and Terri. And that is also how, without knowing it, I suddenly had an authority figure in my life. John is not the kind of guy who wants you living upstairs at his house if he doesn't want to teach you something. I didn't know that when he invited me, otherwise I wouldn't have moved in, but it was true. I lived with him and Terri for four years, and I was there when the next two kids were born, Elle and Cassy. And I was there when they got a dog, and I always took the Christmas picture, and I overheard John and Terri fight, and I—more than once—had to go back to my apartment when they were cuddling a little too intimately on the couch.

What I'm trying to say is, I saw a family. For the first time in my life, I saw what a father does, what a father teaches a kid, what a husband does around the house, the way a man interacts with the world around him, the way a man—just as does a woman—holds a family together.

4

Belonging

What the Eisenhowers Knew

The first thing you will notice when you move in with a healthy family is that they cannot work independently. In the first place, there is too much labor involved in raising kids for anybody to sit on the couch for an extended period of time. They are a unit, like a body with different organs or a car with different working parts. Both John and Terri provided incomes. Terri had a great job at an insurance agency downtown and didn't want to leave because they needed the health benefits. They liked her so much that she worked from home most days, but still she worked. John looked after the kids when Terri was busy or running errands in town, and Terri looked after everything when John was on a trip. But it wasn't just the adults that had important roles. In a way, so did the kids. It was obvious, watching them and being around them, that John and Terri took great delight in their children. They were better than television to them. And the kids felt important, I think, because they would do silly things to make their parents laugh or dangerous things and have John or Terri yelling or talking them down off the balcony railing.

It all reminded me of a book I read a few years ago called *At Ease: Stories I Tell to Friends*. It was written by Dwight D. Eisenhower, the World War II general who became president. I've always been curious about successful men, leaders, and what they know that the rest of us don't. This book was entertaining because Eisenhower was a character, nearly getting himself kicked out of West Point, causing a lot of trouble. But always there was in him a sense of confidence, a sense he would become somebody important. And more than this, he believed the world *needed* him—that if he didn't exist, things would fall apart. He believed he was called to be a great man. I wondered, as I read, where he got this confidence.

I found the reason for Eisenhower's confidence early on in the book, in a chapter in which he discussed his childhood. Dwight Eisenhower said that from the beginning, his mother and father operated on an assumption that set the course of his life—*that the world could be fixed of its problems if every child understood the necessity of their existence.* Eisenhower's parents assumed, and taught their children, that if their children weren't alive, their family couldn't function.

If you think about it, it isn't just kids without fathers who don't usually feel important; it's most of us. I mean, can you imagine growing up believing that if you didn't exist, your family would fall apart? Can you imagine how different the world would be if all children were taught this idea?

I found the sentiment striking, and I wondered what it would have been like if, as a kid, I had felt completely needed by my family. My mother needed me, it's true, and she was certainly loving, but she was also burdened with paying bills, working late hours to pay those bills, and managing life as a single parent. For the better part of my childhood, at least on weekdays, my sister and I were left alone. Weekends would have my mother home, and we would take outings, fly kites, go to children's museums and plays. But even this was more stimulation and entertainment for us than it was rest for her. She mothered herself into exhaustion. Weekdays, Mom would work late, often coming home right around our bedtime, and even then we were all too tired to act like a family. I knew, somehow, that my mother's long working hours were because of my sister and me. But I never thought to ascribe my mother's emotional and physical exhaustion to the lack of a husband and father; rather, I ascribed it to my existence. In other words, I grew up learning the exact opposite of what Eisenhower was taught. I learned that if I didn't exist, the family would be better off. I grew up believing that if I had never been born, things would be easier for the people I loved.

A thought like this can cripple a kid. This may sound like so much psychobabble, but to me it's become an obvious truth. If a kid grows up feeling he is burdening the people around him, he is going to operate as though the world doesn't want him. I didn't recognize this feeling in myself until the last few years—my late twenties and early thirties—but it has always been there.

The ramifications of believing something as untrue as this are extensive. Because I believed I was a burden, I would pull out of conversations when they got too personal. And despite the strongest of invitations to connect, I feel, intrinsically, that the other person will eventually be burdened by his or her relationship with me. I find myself doing a great job at small talk, trying to be charming and all, but when it comes time for a person to actually know me, I run for the hills. Any ability I have to be charming also comes from this desire not to be a burden. If I'm light and easy to be around, my community won't want to throw me out.

If you think about it, if you tried to raise a kid to become president one day, you'd probably try to teach him about politics, about how elections work, about government. But Eisenhower didn't learn any of that. What he learned was that the world needed him. Everything else he figured out later. It's no wonder he grew up to become president. If you believe your family will fall apart without you, you probably go on to believe your community will fall apart without you, and then your city and country. And in just about every dynamic you walk into, you would feel the authority to lead, to hold things together, to bring life and service to the people you interact with—just as you had done when you were a kid with your family.

And conversely, you can't blame a kid for feeling un-wanted if his father takes off. If you think about it, God gives a father a specific instinct that makes him love his kid more than anything in the world. I suppose that same in-stinct was floating around in my father's brain, too, but for whatever reason, he took a look at me and split. Even the instinct God gave him wasn't strong enough to make my dad stay. And that has made me feel, at times, there is this detestable person living within my skin who makes people feel as though they must carry me on their backs. Walking through the park one night I realized I was operating out of a feeling of inferiority. Deep inside, I believed life was for other people—that joy was for others, and responsibility was for others, and so on and so on. In life, there were peo-ple who were meant to live and people who were acciden-tally born, elected to plod the globe as the despised.

These thoughts are illogical, I realize. There isn't any proof that a guy who grows up in a family with a good dad is any better than a guy who grows up in a family with a bad one. Still, a logical argument isn't able to change the heart. My mind knew there was nothing wrong with me—that the problem was the message my father handed down—but this *knowledge* didn't make me *feel* any more secure. For many years, all I could do in the healing process was recognize I felt inferior and tell myself this feeling was a lie. For a long time, I couldn't go any further than this.

The continents began to shift during this time with John and Terri. There were times I would watch John interact with Chris and I would get jealous. I'm not saying I was jealous of *Chris*, and I don't even know if jealousy is the word I'm looking for. I only mean I would feel a sense of unfairness. The idea that *I* mattered had not been instilled in me the way John was instilling it in Chris. Chris will never have to learn he matters, or at least he will not have to swim up a stream of lies.

The MacMurray family dynamics allowed me to picture what should have existed in my own life. It's not that I wanted John to pick me up and set me on his lap. But it did make me wonder why God would allow me to grow up without a father saying he loved me or was glad I was around.

It's odd to be talking about this as an adult. But as I've processed the ramifications of growing up without a father, I've realized the incredible hole in my heart this absence has left. I wish my father and I had a friendship and that he would call once every couple weeks and tell me I was doing a good job. I hunger for this. I don't actually like thinking about this stuff, but I have a sense wounds don't heal until you feel them. What I mean is, I could lash out against the world for the rest of my life and never stop to do the hard work of asking why I'm angry or why I feel pain, then come to the difficult truth that the pain is there because I wanted to be loved, and I wasn't. I wanted to be important to my father, but I wasn't. I wanted to be guided, but I wasn't. And then, honestly, to feel whatever it is that hard truth creates—to respond in the way I need to respond.

Not long ago these ideas became emotional for me. It was

the week before Father's Day, and a few of my friends had told me they were planning large dinners or trips to be with their dads. Perhaps it was because I was operating on so little sleep following a trip I'd taken—or perhaps it was because Father's Day is a foreign concept to me, like celebrating relationships with aliens—but on a particular night, I felt my soul collapsing. I was struggling against a writing deadline and feeling, as I often do, that whatever book I write will only hit the world as a burden to its library. I wanted a father to walk through the door and tell me me this wasn't true, that I was here on purpose and I had a purpose, and that a family and a father and even a world needed me to exist to make himself and themselves more happy. And it occurred to me, then, that a father was not going to walk through the door, that there would be no encouragement, there would be no voice of calm, there would be no larger, mature elephant whose presence would correct the stray thoughts in my mind. It occurred to me this would never, ever happen. For the first time in my life, I realized, deep down, I never had a dad.

I don't cry much, but on that night I did. I lost it. I shoved my computer aside and buried my head in my pillow like a child and sobbed. I sobbed for nearly an hour. I hate saying this because it sounds so weak, and I don't like dramatics, but I remember the night quite well, and there was no question something busted open.

Somebody said realizing we are broken is the beginning of healing. And for me, some of the healing began that night.

Because my mom made us go to church when we were kids, I've always been a person who prays. I don't understand why, but I've never had much of a problem talking to God. I haven't always liked reading the Bible or going to church, but I think from an early age God kicked open the door to his office and made sure I know I could barge in at any time. When I started feeling a lot of self-pity about not having a father—when I realized the stuff going on at the MacMurray house had never happened at my house—I started asking God why. My attitude, at first, was quite accusatory. I went to God saying: *You shafted me. Why didn't I get a father to tell me he loved me, to teach me all this stuff?*

I don't think God got offended when I accused him; I think he was understanding. Praying those honest prayers led to a series of epiphanies that helped a great deal. Watching John interact with his son, I realized that what I really wanted, what my soul was longing for, was *belonging*.

—————■—————

I WAS WASHING my car one afternoon when John came out and invited me to go with him to Lost Lake, deep in the Cascade Wilderness. He wanted to shoot a view of Mount Hood from the north. On the drive up, John told a story about the last time he had been to Lost Lake. He had navigated the thin forest service roads on a snowmobile, hoping to photograph the snow on the pines around the banks of the lake and the white cathedral of a mountain reflected in the water.

"No kidding," John said, telling me the story, a cup of lemonade in his free hand and the other gripping the steering wheel, cornering the back country bends about ten miles per hour too fast. "It probably took four hours to get up there. I mean, we've been driving for an hour or more, right, and we've still got half an hour to go."

Waving his cup at the landscape beyond the windshield, John said: "Imagine all of this covered in snow—how long it would take on a snowmobile." He took a drink of his lemonade and turned his head behind him to see if there was any color on the mountain. I could hardly keep myself from reaching over to grab the steering wheel as John slid off the road, pulled the truck back onto the shoulder, and then, without so much as lifting his foot off the gas pedal, turned around again to check the color on the mountain.

"Did you get your shot?" I questioned, squinting and grimacing as 700-year-old trees blurred by only inches from the mirror outside my door.

"Well," John continued, still looking back at the mountain, "I got up there, and of course, the sky was thick with clouds. Nothing. I mean you could see the mountain, but the west was all low clouds and there was no color, nothing to shoot at all. I couldn't believe it, because I was freezing and I had rented this snowmobile, and I was getting pretty frustrated. I kept checking my watch, knowing there were only a few minutes left before sunset."

"And you still had to drive the snowmobile back to the road," I said.

"Exactly. I had another three or four hours to get back, this time in the dark." John shook his head and rolled his eyes as the truck slipped off the road again. He jerked it back while taking a sip of his lemonade.

"No shot, right?" I questioned again, slyly slipping on my seat belt.

"Well," John continued, "I started packing up my gear. I had the camera wrapped up and put away in my bag and was taking down the tripod when, out of nowhere, here comes this shaft of orange light, like at a rock concert." John pointed out the front window as if toward the mountain as he spoke. "I'm telling you," he said, "this incredible light was shining out like heaven split open, all the rays flooding Ladd Glacier, the color mirrored perfectly in the still lake, the snow in the pines all aglow—the whole bit, right? It was like magic or something."

"And you had put your camera away."

"I had put my camera away. Yeah. But I got it out." At this point, John looked right into my eyes, not paying attention to the road. I kept looking out the front window, gripping the dashboard with my fingernails, wondering at what point we were going to drive off a cliff. John must have thought his truck had autopilot, I reasoned, trying to rationalize his insane driving. He took a breath and kept talking, still not looking at the road. He even took his hands off the wheel to motion how, exactly, he unwrapped his camera. Terror was taking over my bodily functions.

"So I unwrapped it, bolted it to the tripod, inserted the film." John started motioning like he was putting film into his camera. I started gasping a little, my fingernails moving from the dashboard to the armrest, my other hand clutching the seatbelt, my eyes feeling like they were crawling back into my head. "Then I focused," he continued, turning his hand like he was turning a knob, "and hit the button." As John said this, he clenched his hand into a fist and tapped his thumb against the other fingers, like a guy with a grenade. He then reached down and picked up his lemonade, put his hand back on the wheel, and steered left no more than two feet from a giant evergreen. I audibly gasped as the branches of the tree scraped the side of the truck. I slipped down into the seat and stared up at the ceiling, breathing out a kind of thanks to God for letting me live through the near miss of the tree, not to mention the cliff a mile back.

"Exactly," John said, shaking his head, responding to my gasp. "I almost didn't get the shot!"

"What shot?" I said, looking at him as though he were crazy.

"The one of Mount Hood. Haven't you been listening?" John shook his head.

"I was listening," I lied, sliding deeper into my seat.

"I'm telling you," he continued, "as soon as I hit that button, the color started to fade, and within a minute, it was all gone. I couldn't believe it. God showed up on that one, for sure."

I slid back up in my seat, hoping John wouldn't launch into another story and forget he had a truck to drive. I composed myself and adjusted the air conditioning vents.

"So you think God did that?" I asked, feeling a bit more comfortable as the road straightened out and started climbing again.

"Do I think God did what? The sunset?" John clarified.

"Yeah, the sunset."

"No, Don. I don't think God did it." My friend shook his head again. "I think Mother Teresa did it."

"Very funny," I said.

"Of course he did it. Who else would have done it? Spielberg? Hiding in the trees with some lasers? It was God!"

"He did it just so you could see it. Just so you could take the shot?" I questioned, the doubt in my voice coming through clear.

"Well, no, I mean I don't think he did it just because I wanted the shot. If that were the case, I would be the greatest landscape photographer on the planet. I'd never have another dud trip for the rest of my life." He was smiling as he said this, as if thinking wishfully.

"So, he did or didn't do it?" I asked, matter-of-factly.

"He did it, but he did it for us."

"Us?" I questioned. "You mean you and me?"

"Us," John stated. "He did it for his children. That is what beauty is for. All this beauty exists so you and I can see his glory, his artwork. It's like an invitation to worship him, to know him."

"You think?" I said, softly, after a reflective pause.

"Absolutely, Don. Beauty doesn't make any sense apart from God giving a gift to his children. Think about it. Is there a Darwinian explanation for beauty? Not really. It's a love letter, that's all. It's this massive letter to creation, inviting us to enjoy him. I'm always telling the kids that sunsets are God's final brushstrokes on the beauty of the day."

"But why would he do that?" I asked.

"Because it is who he is. It's like with Chris," John leaned back in his seat a bit when he thought about his son. "I do things for Chris because I know Chris will love it. We go on a hike, we go down to the river, whatever. Showing Chris things that give him pleasure also gives me pleasure. I've seen a river a thousand times; after a while, you just get bored. But when Chris and I go to the river, I live the whole thing through him. I feel his pleasure, and it gives me pleasure. So, God is like that. A father is a fitting metaphor for God."

"For some," I said cynically, rolling my eyes. John looked over and smirked, but something in his glance evidenced that he suddenly remembered I didn't have a dad. I wasn't trying to make a big deal out of it. John nodded a little and hummed, though and grabbed the steering wheel like he was thinking about something. It was a long time after that until he talked again.

Once we got up to Lost Lake, he told a story about the time he took a canoe out to try to get another angle on the mountain, then he pointed out clouds he thought might light up come sunset, but it wasn't until we hiked around to the south side of the lake and were standing on the dock that John brought up our previous conversation. And I've come back to what he said many times. He was setting up the tripod and opening the camera case, and he started talking, not really looking at me.

"You know, Don," he said, fidgeting with a lens, snapping it into the camera, and setting the whole thing atop the tripod, "sometimes I don't even think of the kids as my own kids."

I thought about that for a second. "Terri sleep with the mailman?" I joked, more or less under my breath.

"Very funny," he said, shaking his head. "I ought to throw you in the lake for that one."

"Kidding," I told him.

"I mean they are *our* kids and all," John sounded introspective as he talked, absorbed in thought while he adjusted the camera, "but really they belong to God. Terri and I had sex, but that's it. I don't know how to make a human being. God makes a human being."

"Why do you bring this up?" I asked after a minute or so of silence.

"I guess what I'm saying is, one day, I've got to introduce Chris to his real Father. And I'm not talking about the mailman." I laughed as John delivered that line. "I mean God put me in Chris's life," he continued, "to take care of him and love him, but ultimately, we all belong to God. In Scripture he refers to himself as our Father, and I think he really longs for us to know him as that. So I would say, none of us is really without a father." Again, John didn't look at me as he talked. He started focusing his camera and reading his light meter. He cupped his hands above his eyes and checked the west for color.

"Point taken," I said, mostly to break the silence.

"I don't know, Don, maybe you have to be a father to understand it. And I think someday you will understand it. But there isn't any love like this. I love Chris and the girls in a way I can't explain. I really can't. It feels like some kind of miracle. I want them to love life; I want to give them joy; I want them to mature. And now that I have felt all this, I understand so much more of life; I understand why a sunset is beautiful; I understand why I don't get what I want all the time; I understand why God disciplines me; I understand God is a father."

At this point, some color spilled out of the west, brightening the rolling hills of evergreen, and fell across Ladd Glacier. John didn't say anything, he just pointed at the water. And in the water I could see the mountain perfectly mirrored, the point of its summit, the black crag of rock rising up like a spine on the south face. John pressed his thumb against the trigger and reached in his bag for another slide, slipping the exposed plate out of the camera and replacing it with a new one. He waited a second, checked the upside-down image in the viewer, then snapped another picture. After this, the brilliant color faded into light purples and amethyst. John took one more shot of the less brilliant light, and then we sat on the dock and watched the sky slowly go dark.

On the drive back to the house, John was quiet. I started thinking about God as father, wondering whether I really believed it. I had always believed God was loving and kind; and as I said before, prayer came easily to me. But, honestly, I had a more distant picture of God than that of father. The God in my imagination was terribly old, forgetful, not so much interacting with humanity as apathetically watching us work our jobs and mow our lawns. This idea of God fathering us was new to me, and while I confess I liked it, I didn't know if I could buy in. Maybe John was right; maybe I had to actually be a father before I could understand. But I liked the bit of hope. I liked the idea of God, up in heaven, offering guidance and counsel and reward in my life. And I liked the idea I hadn't been completely abandoned.

About the time John and I came off the forest service road, back onto the highway that snakes down Mount Hood, I remembered a commercial that used to run on television when I was a kid. It was a Lifesavers commercial that had a boy sitting on the side of a hill with his father. The father and son were watching the sunset, and as the sun descended, the father whispered to his son, "Going, going, going," and as the sun finally slipped beneath the horizon, the father whispered: "Gone." Then this kid, silhouetted in the evening light, looked up at his father and said: "Do it again, Dad."

It had been ten years since I had seen that commercial,

but thinking about the things John said and having watched purple slip down the glaciers on Mount Hood, the mountain laying its reflection against the water, I wondered about God as Father, about how he might get joy by giving us joy, the way John said he experienced this with Chris.

The idea became more appealing as we continued driving home, because if it were true, it meant I did belong, that *all* of us belonged, that we're here on purpose. And though some of us grow up without biological fathers, none of us grows up without our actual Father. That is, if we have skin, if we have a heart that is beating and can touch and feel, then all this is because God has decided it would be so, because he wanted to include us in the story.

By the time we got back to the house, Terri and the kids were asleep. John and I sat in the den and watched *Sports Center* for a while. During commercials, he would mute the television and make small talk about some of the trips he had coming up, wondering out loud how he was going to get around once arriving in New Zealand, wondering how many days he should spend there as opposed to Australia. He was saying all this with some regret, and you could tell he didn't like being away from his family. But during the last commercial break, he started talking again about being a father, and I could tell he was doing it more for me than just to reminisce. He told me that when Terri gave birth to Chris and he held his son in his arms for the first time, it was the closest he had ever been to understanding the love of God. He said that though he had never met this little person, this tiny baby, he felt incredible love for him, as though he would lie down in front of a train if he had to, that he would give up his life without so much as thinking about it, just because this child existed. John set this love beside other relationships, but they didn't compare. In other relationships, the person he knew had to earn his love. Even with his own father, John *learned* to love him, and with his wife, they had *fallen* in love over several years, becoming closer and closer friends. But it wasn't that way with his children. His love for them was instantaneous, from the moment of their birth. They had performed nothing to earn his love other than be born. It was the truest, most unconditional love he had known. John said if his love for Chris was the tiniest inkling of how God loved us then he had all the security in the world in dealing with God, because he knew, firsthand, what God's love toward him felt like, that it was complete.

"I'm just saying, Don, if God is our Father, we've got it good. We've got it really good." After that, John tossed the remote into my lap, put his glass in the sink, and said good night.

"See you in the morning," I said.

"Good night, Don," John said, the kitchen door closing behind him.

5

Spirituality

God Is Fathering Us

It feels creepy to say God is fathering us—creepy in an invasion of privacy sense. I mentioned before that prayer comes easily to me, but I confess I like the distant God, the God who has a firm grasp of physics but isn't so swift at relational dynamics. I see God this way most of the time, as a kind of foggy-minded scientist who never got married: too smart, really, to "get" people. You don't picture God being good with women, do you? Or sitting around at a baseball game smoking a cigar, talking about the time the ball went through Buckner's legs.

I've always thought of God in conceptual terms, the way Brian Greene thinks about superstrings. Still, I find this sad. God couldn't make it more clear that he wants intimacy. In Bible study once, John explained how strongly God communicates his desire for relationships. He calls himself a bridegroom, a friend, a lover, a shepherd. An Old Testament book called Song of Songs is ripe with erotic imagery, and if you take it allegorically, it makes you wonder if God doesn't want us to be, somehow, spiritually wooed.

But God lives in heaven, not down the street. He can't play with us, as it were. I confess I often think of God like "the boy in the bubble" trying to explain to the other kids that while they can't play basketball with him, exactly, they can still talk on the phone about comic books or something. I know I'm trivializing God, and I don't mean to, but it does feel like his bigotry against our sin-germs affects his ability to bond.

But the stuff John said about God fathering us stayed with me. John went overseas for a time, shortly after our conversation, and I started wondering how, if God wanted to father us, he could do so from such intangibility. What I mean is, how does the owner and creator of the hamster cage interact with the hamsters? How could an interaction with God look anything like the interaction we're supposed to have with our earthly fathers? And worse, if our earthly fathers are God's way of communicating his love for us, then apparently, God only loves some of us. And the way the statistics are going, fewer of us every day.

Then I began to wonder if I was pushing the father metaphor too far, that perhaps the metaphor's purpose is more humble. I wondered if all the relationships we have— relationships with our lovers, our mothers, our friends—are not unlike blurred photos of our relationship with God, as though they are foreshadowings in the sappy prologue of an eternal novel.

I wondered if sliding our arms around a woman's hips wasn't a kind of infantile introduction to the metaphysical. If I allow myself, I can see God holding up flashcards as I fall in love with a woman, cards that say, *this is love, I'm like this love, only better.*

"See," God says, pointing at the flashcard with the word "love," then pointing at his own chest while I move down the woman's lips to her chin and her neck. "See," God says, putting down the flashcard with "love" and picking up the word "oneness." He says: "Get it? Do you see? It's all living metaphors. It's a hint of oneness—like my Trinity."

Thinking about this for too long made me dizzy. But I admit I started getting used to the idea of calling God "Father." I was ready for God to step out of anonymity. I wanted to know that what John had said was true, not only as a guy who grew up without a dad, but as a human being. And as odd as all the metaphor talk may sound, thinking of human love as a metaphor for who God is helped me. It helped me know he is doing what he can for us, and it helped me realize I probably know as much about God as a baby knows about the physics of the mobile dangling above his crib.

After all, the metaphors—love between a father and a son, between a man and a woman—didn't have to be exact. They were only supposed to make a motion, to *grunt* toward the inexplicable. And we don't *all* get to experience *all* the metaphors. A person who never leaves China doesn't get to appreciate God's handiwork in Yosemite National Park, but he will have his own versions there in China. This was important to me, because it meant that, even though I didn't have a dad, I still knew about love, and from plenty of places. So, while all the metaphors weren't firing, some of them were. I could still understand that God was loving and kind, because I knew about love and kindness. And I could still understand him as the Father to the fatherless, even if not firsthand.

What I'm getting at is that the concept of a father may have been soiled for some of us, but it was important for me to realize who did the soiling. To be fair, it wasn't God. If I take the Bible as true, then God bears none of the negative characteristics of our biological fathers. And when I think of my own father as a living flashcard rather than a mirror image, I'm comforted that the One toward whom the metaphor grunts is vastly superior to the grunt itself.

So I said this out loud: "I want God to father me." I'm not trying to be pious here, it's just that I knew guys who were truly fathered had certain advantages in life. They were good at sports, for example, and good with girls. They knew how to manage money better and got their college paid for. At least some of them. So I wanted this, and even though God lived in a bubble, I wanted him to step out of heaven and show me how to work a power saw.

I prayed about it a little, but God never showed up. He

never knocked on my door with a football under his arm, big smile from ear to ear. So I started feeling stupid for wanting him to father me in the first place. But a few things happened that helped me understand God, how he works, who he is, and that in a way, he had been fathering me all my life. I know it all sounds like mushy new age spirituality, like I ought to be living in a tent out in Colorado, asking a tree what I should eat for breakfast, but I'm not like that. I don't think he fathers us by putting vague notions in our minds, or talking to us through whispery winds. I'm speaking in very practical terms.

John's mentioning how God worked something like a father led me on a search through the Bible. It wasn't a very deep search, because I don't know the Bible very well, but the searching I did proved worth the time. And perhaps it's just me, but it seems like no matter where I looked in the Bible, I could see God was fathering people, or doing something very much like fathering people.

The first thing I found was in the Book of Romans. Paul, when he started the book, began by talking about people who decided not to have anything to do with God, and because of that, they'd all become pagans, not really knowing how to control themselves, not having any discipline. They didn't know how to be humans, really. And in a way, I knew I was kind of like those guys. I'm not evil by today's standards, and I'd not done or even thought to do many of the things Paul was talking about, but in general I felt like one of those guys because they were a bunch of people who were disassociated from their father. And when I say Father here, I'm talking about God.

It made me think of those elephants again and how they needed a bigger, older elephant to change their biochemistry and teach them how to be who they were. I wondered if this wasn't, basically, what Paul was getting at in the Book of Romans. Without God being God in our lives, we are going to mess it up somehow. I guess I'm also saying that we are interdependent.

It only makes sense. People who go out in the woods by themselves for a long time usually come back crazy. And it's also true that men become who they were designed to be when they interact with a woman, and vice versa for that matter. Having kids brings about another kind of maturity, too. Relationships unlock certain parts of who we are supposed to be. I think one of the things Paul might have been saying in Romans is that being in a relationship with God helps us understand who we are and become who we are designed to become. And so in a way, it seemed like God was supposed to be the bigger, older elephant to those guys who were messing everything up in Rome. And the reason they were messing up their lives was because they didn't want anything to do with him.

———— ■ ————

IT HELPED ME to consider this dynamic in natural terms. About this time, I was planting a couple tomato plants in the backyard. I'd never planted anything before, but the guy across the street had planted some tomato plants the year before and that got me interested. I was digging a little hole and sticking the starter plant in the ground when the miracle of the process occurred to me. All you do is stick a plant in the dirt, and the sun and soil and a summer's worth of time turns the tomato plant into a living salad maker. Its DNA is activated by outside forces, so it becomes what it is supposed to become only in the right elements.

It's like it says in the Bible, if we know God and interact with him, we are like a tree firmly planted by a river. And I started wondering if God fathering us, and our paying attention to him and obeying him, wasn't the process we go through to produce fruit, or to become what we are supposed to become. Just like my tomato plant, for example.

But what does this look like? That's when I came across a copy of the Lord's Prayer. It was on a refrigerator magnet at a friend's house. Because I had been thinking about the fatherhood of God, the word Father stuck out, and I stood and read through it while I was getting some water. The prayer goes like this:

Our Father, Who art in heaven,
Hallowed be Thy name.
Thy kingdom come, Thy will be done
On earth as it is in heaven.
Give us this day our daily bread.
Forgive our transgressions

Even as we have forgiven our enemies.
And lead us not into temptation
But deliver us from evil.
For Thine is the kingdom and the power and the glory
   forever. Amen.

I liked the fact Jesus said we could call God Father. And even though I had read that passage many times before, in this new light it felt revolutionary. Since I was a kid, I had always thought that passage was only about Jesus's attempt to teach people to pray. At my church, we would read the passage as though there were supposed to be little check boxes next to each idea you were to cover when you talked to God. I figured if I covered all (or perhaps some) of those checks, then my prayer would get through more clearly, and God would respond. It was like having the correct e-mail address. I still think something like this is true, but I wonder if there isn't more.

I read the passage again and saw that Jesus was talking to a mixed group of religious people. Some were Jews, who believed a person interacted with God by obeying a system of laws. Others were Gentiles, the non-Jews. These guys, according to Jesus, were interacting with God as though he were a kind of good-luck charm. Jesus said their prayers went on and on as endless rambling. It struck me that Jesus wasn't so much teaching people to pray as reminding them that God wants us to relate to him in a personal way. Maybe Jesus was teaching that prayer wasn't just about behavior but about perspective. He was saying they should relate to God as he has always related to them, as their father. Christ was giving us a beginner's course on how to do this. He was showing us what God does as a Divine Father, and what we should do as his children.

This revelation radically reshaped the way I think about and interact with God.

When Jesus said we should go into our inner room and shut the door, that meant God wanted to be intimate with us.

In a way, Jesus was countering the trend of the time to pray loudly and in public as a way of getting other people to think we were godly. I guess back in the day women thought that was sexy or something. But praying loudly and publicly reduced God to a vague impersonal deity of rules and rituals. This view didn't interest Jesus at all. In sharp contrast to the religious norm, Jesus's use of the word Father is unreserved and strong.

Another thing I noticed about Jesus's prayer is that he submitted to God: "Thy Kingdom come, Thy will be done, on Earth as it is in Heaven," Jesus says. And I don't think Jesus was saying God was a control freak, trying to make himself feel powerful. He could do that by smashing atoms together if he wanted; rather, in asking us to submit it seemed to me Jesus was saying, Look, you are going to want to do things your way, but your way isn't the best for you. Trust me, I know what you need. Jesus said this outright in his lead-in to the prayer: he said our Father in heaven knows what we need before we even ask him.

I know submitting to authority isn't the most popular thing to do these days, but the thing about fathers, at least in John MacMurray's case, is they always have their kids' interests at heart. That concept alone changed everything for me. If God was fathering me, and he knew exactly what I needed, then when I didn't get something I wanted, I could trust God didn't give it to me because it was not something I needed. I think that is part of what Jesus meant when he said "Thy will be done."

Here is how this idea played out in the MacMurray house. Every evening around six, Terri would set dinner on the table, and the family would sit down to eat. And every night, almost without fail, the kids would start to whine. Unless it was chicken nuggets and French fries, there were going to be problems at dinner. One evening, Cassy, who was quite good at lobbying the family for what she wanted, lay down on the kitchen floor and rolled over in frustration about having to eat whatever it was Terri had prepared. John stood at the corner of the island in the kitchen and watched her, trying not to laugh. She twisted and turned and moaned and complained, but John stood silently, not letting her manipulate him. Finally, Cassy belted out the now famous line: "Dad, how could you do this to me?" John and I covered our mouths and looked away in hysterics.

But here is what is so interesting about that scene. Cassy actually believed what she was saying had merit. The pain and frustration she felt about dinner that night was the same pain and frustration you and I probably feel about not getting the job we want, the car we want, or whatever. Looking back, it struck me how often I have wondered, sometimes out loud to God, *How could you do this to me?*

In the situation with Cassy, John had some choices as a father. He could have thrown the dinner out and cooked up some chicken nuggets and fries. But let's be honest, kids whose parents do this for them end up as evil dictators in small countries. Giving Cassy what she wanted rather than what she needed should not be confused with good parenting. If God was withholding something I wanted, it meant I could trust him rather than mimic Cassy's cry.

Instead, what John did with Cassy was to explain she could roll around on the kitchen floor all day, but she still wasn't going to get her way. She was, in fact, going to stand up, go to the table, and eat with the rest of the family, even if it took all night. He was going to father her toward maturity.

Nobody watching John interact with Cassy would say he was an unloving father. There was no diminished affection between Cassy and John. In fact, his giving Cassy what she needed rather than what she wanted was, in itself, an act of love.

In the Lord's Prayer, after Jesus tells us we need to submit to God, he says that God is going to provide, that we can trust him to give us what we need, even down to the basics of food. To me, that seems to build on what Jesus had just said about trusting God to give us what we need rather than what we want.

"Give us this day our daily bread," Jesus said.

I could be wrong, but I think Jesus is talking about much more than providing food. I think that passage is an acknowledgment of God's ability to provide security. In the years I lived with the MacMurrays, I never encountered Chris out in the woods with his BB gun hunting for dinner. Dinner was always on the table around six, and John and Terri were more than happy to provide.

I was e-mailing an old friend recently, whom I hadn't heard from in about ten years. In the time since we talked, my friend Dean had gotten married and had two children. We exchanged pleasantries for a few e-mails, talking about where we were working and what we had been doing since we last talked, and then I asked him about his family. And in a tender e-mail, Dean explained how much his children had changed his view of himself and his life. He talked about how, on days he did not feel like getting out of bed and going to work, he would hear one of his sons' voices in the hall or giggling from their room, and it was enough to get him into the shower and into his suit. He loved his kids and was motivated to provide for their happiness and health. Their having good food to eat and books to read and movies to see mattered more than his comfort. Dean explained that he wouldn't want it any other way, that what was once mundane (having to work) became beautiful because his motives had changed. And I wondered as I read Dean's e-mail how much of God we see in the heart of a good father, loving and providing for his children.

As I stopped to think about it, even the idea of God providing each day could be seen as an invitation to intimacy. He wants us to depend on him, to lean on him, to realize our smallness in the reality of his bigness. Our provision comes from God, Jesus seems to be saying, and in our asking we are acknowledging the love he displays in his willingness to provide. It was a sobering idea to realize, which I suppose is the reason Jesus wants the concept to come up in our prayers. I felt grateful after thinking about how God provides. It might sound silly to say it, but it made me like God more.

Jesus then goes on to explain that we are to forgive our debtors even as we have been forgiven. Looking at this passage through the lens of a child wondering what his father wants, it seems like Jesus is striking a familiar MacMurray family theme. Unity is huge with John and Terri. They are always telling the kids not to fight. Chris isn't allowed to put Elle's head in the fan, for instance. I don't know how many times I saw John kneel down and put his arms around one of his daughters, whispering in her ear, guiding her through the process of asking and giving forgiveness to one of her siblings. The kids had to learn how to live together. It doesn't come naturally. If they weren't guided in this process, and if it wasn't a family rule, they would become isolated and defensive, and they wouldn't grow into maturity. And so it seemed beautiful that God would want us to get along, to forgive each other and accept forgiveness. And it also seemed beautiful that God wasn't just my Father, concerned with my maturity, but he was *our* Father, concerned with the unity and health of the whole family.

Perhaps I'm reading too much into the Lord's Prayer. But I don't think so. If anything, I think I had been reading too little into it all those years. I think the passage clearly demonstrates a father-child relationship. And, like I was saying, these ideas made me grateful.

The prayer ends with some important praise—an admission, if you will, of who does what in the relationship we have with God. Jesus says: "For Thine is the kingdom and the power and the glory, forever and ever. Amen."

I suppose if I were trying to teach this idea to children, I might simply ask them to pray: "God, you are great big. You are bigger than everything, and that is amazing. You are the one with the power, and you always will be."

———■———

HERE IS HOW this broke down after having thought about it for a long time: I used to feel a kind of hopelessness about life. I assumed life was against me, that whatever bad could happen to a person was going to happen to me. It was as though there was a current I was swimming against. But it was studying this passage that changed some of that thinking. God is fathering me. God is fathering us. I know that if God loves me and wants me to succeed as much as John loves his kids and wants them to succeed, then life cannot be hopeless.

But another idea that occurred to me was I needed to change the way I understand spirituality. What I mean is, I needed to *allow* God to father me. I needed to acknowledge him as Father and submit. Traditional language might use the term repentance. In part, this meant admitting I wanted autonomy from God, admitting I wanted my own way, and asking him to change my heart. One of the issues I deal with having grown up without a father is a kind of resentment at the mention of actually needing a dad. I had to admit I needed one. I had to tell God I wanted him to father me.

One of the most tender and beautiful scenes that would occasionally unfold in the MacMurray house was the calm, quiet peace that would come over one of the children when they were done trying to get their way. Cassy would get up off the floor and walk over to where her dad was and hold out her arms, her face still pouting. Then John would sit down on the couch and hold her and rock her in his arms. If John had scolded Chris about something and sent him to his room, Chris would come out later and walk over to John while he was sitting on the couch and climb into his arms, burying his head in John's neck. Sometimes it was as if the kids were saying they were sorry, not yet old enough to know how to express themselves with words. But at other times, and perhaps more tender times, the kids were still frustrated, still confused about why they couldn't get what they wanted or why they seemed to always be getting into trouble; and the embrace, the coming to John and burying themselves in his arms, was more about feeling his love *in* the confusion, *in* the difficulty, than it was about having moved past it. It was as if they were asking if he still loved them, if the discipline meant there was anything lost in their much-needed relationship with their father. There wasn't. Discipline is what a father does *because* he loves.

––––■––––

HERE'S SOMETHING ELSE I noticed John do with his kids. Chris and Elle were arguing one time, and John felt like he raised his voice too loud in telling them to knock it off. Not long after that, maybe a few minutes, he went to them and told them he was sorry for yelling. They didn't seem to care, and it wasn't a big deal, but for some reason it stuck in my mind as an interesting thing for a father to do. I asked him about it the last time we talked, and John said he tries to apologize when he messes up as a dad, letting his kids know they are more important to him than his pride. He kind of laughed and admitted he screwed up fairly often. But then he said something I thought was pertinent to those of us who grew up without dads. John said another reason he apologized was because he didn't want his kids to have any negative perceptions about God. He said that the way a kid feels about his or her dad is sometimes projected onto God, so if he apologized when he messed up as a father, the kids would know that was his mistake, and didn't have anything to do with who God is. Or at least that is what he hoped.

I liked that idea, because it reaffirmed that our fathers aren't God. They can help us understand who God is and how good he is, but they can also do a lot of damage. God is God regardless, and if we take the Bible as true, it's good to think he is fathering us perfectly.

There is this great text in the Bible that says, essentially, if our earthly fathers know how to love us, just imagine how great God's love is. I take this to mean that even a very good earthly father is no comparison to God.

There is a part of me, and I think it is a growing part, that believes if I submit to God, read the Bible and obey his commands, and talk to him about stuff going on in my life, in his own way, he is fathering me toward maturity.

And there is something profoundly humbling about knowing God. I'm not talking about the trinket God or the genie-in-a-lamp God, I mean the God who invented the tree in my front yard, the beauty of my sweetheart, the taste of a blueberry, the violence of a river at flood. I think there are a lot of religious trends that would have us controlling God, telling us that if we do this and that and another, God will jump through our hoops like a monkey. But this other God, this real God, is awesome and strong, all-encompassing and passionate, and for reasons I will never understand, he wants to father us.

6

Authority

The Thing about Choppy Air

When I was younger, I didn't trust older men. And it's only in the last few years I've understood why. I know I was more or less an awkward kid growing up, a few years behind in maturity, always having some kind of show-off show going on, and I don't think a lot of the men I knew back then had a great deal of tolerance for me. My grandfather died when I was a kid, and my dad, of course, had taken off before I was old enough to walk. Then one of my uncles left my aunt, and my other uncle had kids of his own to raise on the other side of the country, so the immediate family had no men at all. No men and no boys, just me and a lot of women.

Being a guy, of course, I felt out of place; but I didn't feel any more comfortable standing around with a group of

men, either. When hanging out with my friends and their
dads, I knew I didn't belong. There is something about having your own father standing there talking to your friends'
fathers that validates you—you're *his* kid, not just some
stray that wandered in off the street. So, although I never
knew it at the time, I grew up with a constant feeling of in-
security, even a fear that there was a consequence for being
who I was, a kind of subconscious knowing that I wasn't
okay and that someday I was going to pay for it. This feeling
I didn't fit in gave me a noticeable distrust of authority, especially of older men.

Sometimes I think the reason we don't like certain people
is because we feel insecure around them. We like to chalk it
up to political or philosophical differences, maybe, but the
truth is, if we are honest, we are drawn to those who validate us and affirm us, and we resist those who don't.

Because I didn't have a father, I felt there was a club of
men I didn't belong to. I would have never admitted it at
the time, but I wanted to belong. I desperately wanted to
belong. At the father-and-son campout, I knew Matt wasn't
my dad, and I knew he probably didn't want to be there. I
knew he was slightly embarrassed that in a group of men
who were bonding with their sons, he was walking around
with a charity case. I couldn't have put words to it back
then, but I felt it. Every time I met an older man, I assumed
he would not like me and would not want me around. I felt
as though all the men in the world secretly met in some
warehouse late at night to talk about man things, to have

secret handshakes, to discuss how great it was to have a penis and what an easy thing it was to operate, how to throw a football or a baseball, how to catch a fish and know what kind it was and be able to grab it and stop its flapping around, doing this without jolting their heads back or squinting their eyes. They talked about how to look a woman in the eye and tell her she was your woman and that she looks good in that dress and make it so your eyes say you love her but you could survive without her, and how to drive a stick-shift truck without grinding the gears. And then I secretly believed that at the end of the meeting, they gathered around and reminded each other that under no circumstances was anybody to tell *me* about these things.

Absurd, I know. I say this because when you grow up believing an entire community of men have a fraternity you are not allowed into, you don't like them, or their club, and you tend to defend your manhood by awkwardly trying to knock up cheerleaders. Or you try to become a man by getting into fights in bars. Or you just give up completely and silently harbor bitterness toward the idea of manhood all together. And you hate men who look anything like authority. You hate them because they first hated you.

Sometimes I think if people have parents who speak love into their life, they end up with a personality that trusts others more easily, feels more comfortable, gives and takes with authority and so on. There is a good chance you and I didn't learn that trust. I've thought a lot about why I struggled so much with authority, and the best reason I've come up with is that the insecurities I felt were compounded by the tone of impersonal indifference I sensed coming from positions of power. The natural reaction to indifference is resistance, cynicism, bitterness, hurt, and so on; and without a father figure representing positive authority, all authority became suspect, and communication with the God-given guides became strained.

I didn't show this mistrust on the surface. I could get along pretty well, but the bitterness was there, deep, and it affected things quite negatively. If I were working for a man, for example, and he came out and barked some orders at me and then went back into his office, I would spend the rest of the day imagining myself walking off the job. I would assume at the beginning of the relationship, the guy thought I was a loser and couldn't measure up. A normal kid with a healthy identity would probably jump to the task and earn the guy's respect, really show him he is a man, because he *knows* he is a man. In those instances, however, I would end up loafing around trying to get away with being paid without working. I'm not proud of it now, but I didn't know any better. What I mean is, this is who I thought I was.

As I grew older, the condition got worse. I organized my life so I didn't have to submit to anybody and even found myself getting angry with any man who wanted to impose rules. And when you grow up in a church, there are a million men who want to impose rules. Throw a rock and you will hit a guy looking down his nose at some other guy who isn't "acting right." And I think I assumed anybody twenty years older who wanted to tell me what to do just wanted to use me so he could feel powerful.

In my life, there has never been a connection between authority and love. Even with John MacMurray, who was certainly an authority figure, I didn't find the kind of love I needed. A father is a father is a father, and there isn't any substitute. I would get mad at John, bitter sometimes, and I never knew why. He would ask me to do something, to take out the trash or whatever, and as soon as he left the room the anger would surface in my chest, feelings of bitterness and resentment, and I wanted nothing more than to dump the can of trash on the front lawn.

That was really the beginning of some hard and dark thinking for me. I didn't want to admit I had a problem with authority. And even in the times when I could admit it, those same difficult feelings were there—that the very people who were handing down advice didn't like me, didn't have a stake in whether or not my life was going to turn out well. There was certainly no love, not deep love, not unconditional love.

Everything intensified during the years I lived with John and his family. I haven't told you everything. There were times I hated John. And it's not like he had a bunch of rules or anything. John barely had any rules. But, like I was saying, I operated out of this sense of rejection, unable to understand that John was not my father and wasn't supposed to love me like a father.

Of the four years I lived with John and Terri, this is my

single regret. I wish I had known I could have trusted John. That is, I wish I could have respected John and appreciated him *in his place,* as a friend, a mentor, and nothing more. If I could have done this, I would have clearly seen how much he was for me.

If you think about it, this distrust of authority creates a fierce succession of difficulties. If I put myself in John's shoes, he had no choice but to think I was a bad kid. I mean, he was doing everything he could—mentoring me, letting me live at his place, including me in a small way in his family—and yet I was, in many ways, ungrateful. I would magnify any quirk in John's personality, practically demonizing him.

Here is the real truth I'm stammering toward. John Mac-Murray isn't my father. My boss isn't my father. The cop on the street isn't my father. My father split, and that stinks, and none of these guys is going to replace him. And what that means is that they are not responsible to love me un-conditionally, and they aren't responsible to tell me I am a man. Any love or affirmation they give is a gift, but holding them responsible for the insult my father cast down is inap-propriate. The wound I have isn't there because of them.

———■———

I WAS ON a plane a few years ago, flying from Chicago to Portland, and I happened to plug my headphones into the jack on the armrest. On a plane, you can sometimes listen to the radio transmissions coming in and out of the cockpit. I was curious about what pilots say to each other so, like a good geek, I listened for a while. It turns out, most of the transmissions are about weather and whether or not the plane is heading for choppy air. The pilot would radio to a plane that was en route an hour or so ahead of us and get a report on what kind of turbulence they were experiencing; then, he would turn and radio the plane that had just taken off in Chicago to explain what sort of air we were flying through at the moment. The system was primitive, but intelligent. Planes fly from Chicago to Portland all day, and all day they are handing back warnings and forecasts, keeping everybody safe and comfortable.

It occurred to me, listening to the pilots talk to each other, how much this is like life. I know it sounds simple, but at the time, it came as a revelation. I could see it clearly, the fact that in life there are people being born, just as others are passing away. And all the way through, the guys who are twenty years ahead are teaching the guys twenty years behind what kind of weather they will be encountering at whatever stage of life they happen to be living in. And I couldn't help but wonder if, perhaps, my distrust of authority was costing me something.

I started thinking about the wisdom that is handed down when we have authority figures in our lives. We learn a trade by submitting to authority, we learn a work ethic by submitting to authority, we gain an academic life by submitting to authority, and more than any of this, we learn who we actually are by submitting to authority. And when we have earned authority ourselves, we teach others, because for so many years we have been taught. A guy like me, then, who has a resistance to authority, is begging to be useless. What I mean is, he isn't receiving any advice on how to live, and in turn he isn't able to hand advice down to those who are coming behind him. And if he *is* handing down advice, it isn't good advice. I mean it isn't tested and tried by years of experience.

When I made the connection between the pilots passing back information and an older man passing back wisdom to a younger man, I wondered who I was receiving wisdom from. And I couldn't think of one person. Not one. I immediately assumed this was because men in authority didn't like me. But I was getting too old to still believe that.

It took a long time to connect the fact I didn't like authority with the idea that I felt older men were rejecting me, and even longer to realize I was really looking for the kind of validation I should have received from a father, the kind of validation no man is going to give except to his own son. And that's a bum deal for people like you and me.

I realized, however, there is not a secret meeting of men who weren't teaching me the confidential handshake. Men are just men, and half of them are scared and wondering if they are doing life right anyway. I had to ask for a great deal of forgiveness. Once I understood that authority had its place, I started realizing how much I could benefit by seeking advice from those who were in front of me.

I still have some problems with authority, but it's funny how much of the anger has gone away. I've learned to avoid authority figures who aren't submitting to anybody themselves. What good is the wisdom of a man who has nobody speaking into his life? And I've found if you sit down with a man you trust and respect and explain to him that you never learned about some area of life, girls or money, cars or computers, you would be amazed at how honored he is to help. He'll practically pour out his life, for heaven's sake. I sit down every once in a while with men who are twenty and thirty years older than me, and I ask them if they see any blind spots in my life, character flaws and that sort of thing. The answers that come back are always encouraging, and I can hear in the voices of these men, and see in their eyes—they want me to succeed, they want me to make it and to thrive.

I know my father took off a long time ago, but there isn't any reason this should ruin my life more than it has to. It wasn't easy, but I'm hearing the warnings now, and I'm learning to stay clear of choppy air.

7

Manhood

The Right Equipment

Many years ago, I attended something called a Promise Keepers rally. This was an event where thousands of men gathered in a football stadium to shout cheers about how much they loved God. There was more to it than that, of course, but this was the most noticeable characteristic. It was strictly a religious thing, but I liked it. All the men at the Promise Keepers rally were supposed to sign a contract swearing, under God, they would interact with other races, pray all the time, and refrain from yelling at their wives and kids. I went to the rally the second year they were held, back when Promise Keepers was becoming a movement, and even though I didn't have a wife or kid to yell at, I found the event moving. It made me feel like I was working on my manhood, becoming a better person, sitting and listening to lectures and taking notes and scribbling down ideas—actionable steps I could follow that would make my spiritual manhood more pronounced. Each lecture included lists we were supposed to make and instructions on accountability to get the stuff on our lists done. I didn't know becoming a man involved so much paperwork, to be honest. You have to have a Palm Pilot, practically.

The concept of manhood was relatively new to me. Perhaps because I grew up without the consistent influence of any man, I wasn't aware there was a unique identity that only men could feel. I knew we are were stronger, in general, and our lies come more to the surface, but other than this, I didn't know the distinctions. And when I learned about the distinctions, I rather liked them. I felt, in a way, the Promise Keepers rally helped me understand experientially what a man is supposed to do, what a man is supposed to feel like. And I absorbed the rituals, and I cheered with the cheering, and I noted my notes, and all the while felt as though it was a kind of rite of passage. I was a man, I supposed, because I had attended the rally. I had paid my money and the person at the ticket booth did not hesitate in handing me a pass.

But the feeling of manhood was short lived. As part of our agreement with God, we were supposed to be actively involved in a Bible study, which I did not do. There was a Bible study at my church, but there were women in it, which compromised the "manhood" purpose, so I stopped attending. And we were supposed to include black people in our lives, and I was excited about this until I realized I didn't know any black people. When I approached them at the mall and explained my dilemma, they looked at me confused.

In the long run, the experiment was a flop. I do hold out hope, however, that I will never yell at my wife or kids. At present this is easy because I do not have a wife or kids. As a rule, I do not yell at the wives or children of my friends, and I feel this is good practice for a wife and kids of my own, but they say there is nothing like the real thing to test a man's character. Regardless, the Promise Keepers rally left me in a quandary: I was awakened to the idea there was such a thing as a real man, a God's man, a man's man, but since I hadn't kept any of the promises, a growing doubt was seeded that I might not be the real thing. If there is one thing The Promise Keepers rally insinuated, it was that there were real men and fake men. They even sold bumper stickers that stated "Real Men Love Jesus," and as hopeful as I was that I fit this definition, I secretly knew I wasn't a "Promise Keepers" kind of Christian. I wasn't the kind of Christian who was good at keeping rules.

And if I were honest with myself, I would have admitted I didn't know exactly what a man was. The rally taught me what a man does, and how loud a man must cheer, but apart from shallow bumper sticker logic, Promise Keepers didn't define the term. I found myself looking for a general definition. Because if I had a general definition of a man, I would know whether or not I was one.

I attended a church in the suburbs after this and finally
found a men's gathering where they talked about hunting
and eating wild game, and I would sit there feeling like an
idiot, pretending to be amused by stories about shooting
deer, and how somebody's buddy rushed into a cave and
killed a bear while it was sleeping. The truth is I was never
amused. I wasn't even interested. And even though my best
friend Roy and I went fishing a great deal when I was a kid,
I was never that much into it. For me fishing was just something to do with a friend. I never went hunting, either, and
I was not groomed for sports. I liked war movies some, but
I liked human drama movies more, movies like *The Breakfast Club* or *The Karate Kid*—movies where geeks prevailed
against great social odds so they could date cheerleaders. So
when all the football analogies started up at the men's group,
and all the talk was about how, in our spiritual lives, we are
like characters in the latest bloodfest movie, except we only
get to kill people metaphorically, I just wasn't feeling it. I
continued wondering if I was one of the guys, wondering if
I was really a man. I wondered why they couldn't speak to
somebody on my level. I thought, for example: Why not
have a men's meeting where we talked about how Duckie
got to kiss Molly Ringwald in *Pretty in Pink*, and how someday we were all going to kiss Molly Ringwald, metaphorically?

I knew if we were to break into small groups and the guys
were to start telling stories about how faith is like killing a

sleeping bear, my contribution about how faith is like the last Cure record wasn't going to motivate anybody.

And so for a long time I wandered around in a fog. Manhood felt like something that had been handed to me accidentally. I just knew somebody was going explain I was actually a lesbian with a penis, and if I wanted I could continue to watch college football, but should probably tone down the interest in postseason baseball, as this territory was reserved for men who had killed sleeping bears. Or for men who loved Jesus.

But feelings of rejection always turn into feelings of resentment, and shortly I began begrudging the fact I was made to feel unmanly. I started thinking about how stupid you would have to be to believe life is like an *Alien* sequel and Jesus was like a boxer with a Philadelphia accent. I couldn't sit through men's meetings anymore without rolling my eyes, or, at the end of prayers, sarcastically replacing the common phrase "amen" with a loud and guttural "git 'er dun." I mockingly wore NASCAR shirts to the meetings and made up stories about how I had spent the last two days stalking squirrel on the Pacific Crest Trail. "Them's tasty critters," I'd say in my best hick accent. "Common squirrels keep fat off so they can balance on telephone lines, but mountain squirrels can get big as housecats. . . ."

To my surprise, my commodity rose at Bible study and I was soon asked to teach. I did a series called *The Cheerleaders Are in the Wrong End Zone!* about how sluts in the Bible brought down godly men. You can't fake shallow manhood for long, though, and pretty soon the pastor discovered I had the whole John Hughes collection on DVD and suspended me from teaching indefinitely.

Once again, I felt excluded.

I began to wonder, though, if there wasn't some kind of male spirit God put in a man that was more general— something that would include men who had killed sleeping bears, for sure, but also the rest of us. I knew none of this was scientific, but here's what I meant: Women have a kind of general spirit, very sweet and kind, beautiful like a flower. In a guy there is something else, more like the spirit of a tractor or a calculator. And moreover, I wondered how that spirit was confirmed, how a person knew he had it.

———■———

I TOLD YOU already that my best friend when I was a kid was named Roy. Roy's father was a man's man, a fisherman who worked the oil rigs in the gulf of Mexico. He had an enormous orange tool container out in the backyard, a steel contraption so heavy you needed a forklift to move it. Roy and his father would stay in the backyard 'til all hours, working on their boat or fixing their car. The inside of Roy's house belonged to his mother, so it always smelled like roses or peanut butter cookies, but the backyard belonged to the men, and it smelled like oil and dead fish. I used to go over and sit on a tire to talk to Roy while he lay under his dad's car, handing his father tools. And even though Roy was a couple years younger than me, he seemed to have a kind of knowing, a knowing that if he were asked to do something only a man could do, he could do it. It was a knowing I didn't have, the knowing I discovered I didn't have at the Promise Keepers rally. I know now that the reason Roy had the knowing and I didn't have the knowing was because he had a father to confirm his manhood. I found from experience you can't pick up the knowing at a Promise Keepers rally or at a wild game dinner. You need something more.

The idea that manhood is passed down from father to son has been an unpleasant thought. A writer named John Eldredge talks about this in his book *Wild at Heart*. He says we all carry a "father wound," and unless our father convinces us we have what it takes, we are probably going to flounder for a while. The first time I read *Wild at Heart* I threw it across the room. I hated that book and hated anybody who told me I was less of anything because I grew up without a father. My roommate at the time loved the book, though, and on a long walk home from a coffee shop one night, he kindly explained that the book goes on to talk about how God wants to heal the father wound, and how our identity as men comes from him, how he steps in when our fathers step out. I picked it up again and read through it intensely. I won't go into the book for you here, but it's a good read and I highly recommend it. What I want to talk about, though, is how I got the knowing without getting it from my father.

The thing I believe about manhood now is that it lives within the male from a very early age, and sometimes it gets awakened, and sometimes it doesn't. It doesn't matter how old you are—a man is a man is a man.

I used to think manhood began in your late fifties, that until then it was okay to sit around and play video games, but I saw something a few years ago that changed my mind. My mom used to go into the ghettos south of Houston to bring bubble gum to underprivileged children. She would get a bucket of bubble gum and on Saturday, in all that unbelievable heat, would go door to door to trailers where migrant farm worker families set up makeshift homes—boards leaning against barns, broken-down vans with mattresses where the seats were supposed to go, trailers half ripped apart by hurricanes, the smell of poverty. Mom would go looking for kids, handing them a piece of bubble gum, then she would tell their parents, in whatever Spanish she could muster up, that she wanted to come back the next morning and take the kids to church. She was going to come by in a bus, my mom would say, and they should be standing near the road. The next day mom would take an old school bus and pick up a load of kids, sometimes more than seventy on one bus, then take them back to the church and teach them about the Bible.

One Saturday I went with her to visit a family whose trailer had been destroyed by fire. The family was in the process of moving into another trailer, a tiny thing that was to house more than ten people. My mother heard the family needed a washing machine, and was working to have one delivered. We walked up to the house and were greeted by a child perhaps ten years old. Within seconds, though, I could tell this was no ordinary child. I felt in his handshake and in the confidence of his voice that he was an equal. He stood at the top of the steps and told his little sisters, who were playing in the yard, to stay out of the mud. He talked to them with the authority and kindness of a father. The boy's mother came to the door and he translated for her in Spanish, explaining this was the woman who was going to bring the washing machine. The boy told his mother he would take care of the delivery and she shouldn't worry about it, then turned to thank my mother and me, explaining this was something they needed and it would help the family immensely. I completely forgot we were dealing with a child.

I immediately began to wonder about my own immaturity at this age. When I was this child's age I spent my time fishing in the creek by the railroad tracks or playing video games. In my teenage years, my greatest concerns were whether or not I fit in at school or if my car was cool. I rode an emotional roller coaster, wondering if I was going to fail a test I hadn't studied for.

And it was remembering this kid that caused me to disagree with the whole "Real Men Love Jesus" shtick. The kid may have loved Jesus, I have no idea, but it was at that moment I realized a lot of people are misled by believing they aren't a man unless they read some book or walk through some steps or subscribe to some religion. Don't get me wrong: I happen to be somebody who has realized I need Jesus, and I have even come to love Jesus, but I don't think somebody who doesn't love Jesus is any less of a man than somebody who does. I don't think being a "real man" has anything to do with loving Jesus at all anymore than being a ferret has something to do with riding a bicycle.

I spent a lot of time believing I wasn't a man because I didn't like football analogies, or because I didn't want to put a cheesy bumper sticker on my car, or, well, because I didn't have a father. In a way, the guys who are promoting this approach to manhood are pretty innocent. I realize they are just trying to keep guys from yelling at their wives. But when those tactics hit my insecurities, they created a twinge. Tell a guy who grew up without a father that he is not a man unless . . . and he will automatically assume he isn't one. I didn't need manipulation. I needed affirmation.

The conclusion I have come to is more logical than emotional. It isn't my fault my dad split, and it isn't my fault my identity as a man had never been affirmed. I had to believe in the face of doubt. I had to accept the terms "man," "manliness," and "manhood" as biological terms, and while the sales tactics played on emotions, what I had to focus on was facts. Here's what I mean:

I was asked to speak to a group of nine hundred guys a couple of years ago. They were in high school, mostly, so I started the session by asking the group what a real man was.

"How would you define a real man?" I asked the group, all of them sitting quietly. A hand slowly went up.

"A real man is somebody who provides for his family," the kid said, rather sheepishly.

"Okay, that is good," I confirmed. "That is something a 'good' man does, but I don't think you have to do that to be a real man. Anybody else?"

"A real man is honest; he doesn't lie!" a kid shouted out.

"Very good. But again, I would say this is something a good man does, but not a qualifier for what makes a man a man. Who else wants to play?"

"A real man drives a truck!" a kid shouted out sarcastically. The group laughed.

"Not the qualifier I'm looking for," I laughed back.

The group got quiet for a while as it was obvious they weren't coming up with the right answer.

"Okay," I said, "Take out a sheet of paper, because I am going to give you the definition of a real man. And you are going to want to come back to this over the next several years, because there are going to be times when you will wonder whether you are a real man, and here is a sure way to find out." After I said this I waited for everybody to get out their pens.

"Let me give you God's definition of a real man. I have searched through the Bible, and I have thought a great deal about it, and I think I have come up with the perfect qualifier. If you have this thing, then, according to God, you are a real man." The group looked at me anxiously, some of them knowing, intrinsically, that whatever I said, they would be up for the job, and some of them, quite honestly, looked at me knowing whatever I said would exclude them.

"God's definition of a real man . . ." I said, motioning for them to write it down.

". . . is . . ." I continued.

". . . a person . . ." and I paused dramatically, waiting for everybody to catch up.

". . . with . . ." I said, pausing again, preparing the room for the last line, the ultimate qualifier of a man, the sure sign that God in heaven had spoken, that God in his infinite wisdom and perfection had endorsed them as men.

". . . a person with . . ." I repeated, waiting again until every eye was looking at me, and then I let the cat out of the bag.

". . . a penis!"

And as I said this, jaws dropped. Some of the kids in the back immediately started snickering, kids on the front row looked at me confused, some of the adults in the room dropped their pencils. And then, slowly, the snickers in the back of the room turned to laughter, and the laughter made its way to the front.

And as much fun as I was having, I was also being serious. It had been a long journey for me, a journey filled with doubt and fear, and the only answer I could come up with is that all the commercials, all the sales tactics that said I wasn't a real man unless I bought some book or wore some aftershave or slept with some cheerleader, were complete lies. If you have a penis, I told the group of guys, God has spoken.

I told the story of the kid from the ghetto back in Houston who was leading his family, and how whatever it is God puts in a man has been in all of us since we were young, and how the wealth of our country has caused something called "suspended adolescence," so that some of us haven't stepped into the truth that we are men—instead we are still living like children. But what I really wanted everybody in the room to know was that they were men. So I told them. I asked them to look me in the eye, and I told them, "You are men. Some of you have never heard this before, but I want to tell you, you are men. You are not boys, you are not children, you are not women, you are men. God has spoken, and when God speaks, the majority has spoken. You are a man."

I normally don't get so preachy, but I knew how painful the journey could be, and how some guys will never really believe. I found out later that more than half the guys at the event were not living in a home with their biological fathers. There's no telling what kinds of messages they were getting about who they really were.

The hard truth is, though, just because God made us men doesn't mean we are done. I know the journey of a man is difficult, and that there are forces that are always against us. I enjoy reading books about manhood, as long as they don't use manipulative sales talk. There are a number of books on this subject by guys who are actively trying to help us understand this journey. There will be times reading these books when we are tempted to believe we don't have what it takes, but I doubt very seriously any author is trying to create an exclusive club that cuts us out of membership. How to navigate the journey of manhood is not something I know more about than these guys do, but I think it bears repeating that if God has spoken, the journey belongs to you and me as much as it belongs to a man who grew up with a father. And it's a journey we are on whether we like it or not.

For me, the idea God has spoken is an enormous relief. If I begin to doubt my manhood, if I doubt I have what it takes, I simply have to duck into the nearest bathroom and check my shorts. If God has spoken, then I have within me whatever it takes to do the things a man needs to do, to become a good man for a woman, for some kids, for an office, for whatever it is God wants me to do.

8

Making Decisions

How to Stay Out of Prison

M y friend Travis told me a year ago he has a fear he will some day go to prison. Till then, I had never met anybody besides me with this same fear. Travis doesn't get into trouble, and I don't get into much trouble either, but both of us have a fright that one day we are going to get locked up. With me, it's mostly been about traffic tickets and not paying taxes.

I didn't pay taxes for a few years. I started making some money and finally sat down with an accountant to fill out the forms, but even with her help it was pure torture. I can't stand forms. And I used to be terrible about paying traffic tickets, not because there are forms involved but because this involves writing a check, which is a kind of form. I've had my car towed more times than I can count. I used to get tickets in the mail, notices and things, and I remember thinking that if I didn't actually open the envelope, then the ticket wouldn't apply to me. That's not exactly what I thought, but I sort of *felt* this was true. The letters would find piles on my dresser or next to my bed, and I wouldn't pay attention to them.

Most people like me get married and their wives help them with that stuff, but I'm not married and none of the women I know want to go through my mail. I never went to jail for any of this, but I always thought I might, and I still have a fear my past will come knocking on the door wearing a uniform and holding an outstanding warrant from Kansas or that weekend in Georgia.

I'm still somewhat irresponsible, but it isn't as bad as it used to be. I forget to pay a credit card bill every once in a while, but I do all the big stuff. You can automate most of this these days, but that is hardly the point. I learned to make good decisions.

What I'm saying is there had to come a point when I started taking responsibility for my life. I had to start opening envelopes, even if I didn't feel like it. I had to, because if I didn't I knew I would become one of these guys whose car is filled with newspapers and fast-food wrappers and stuffed animals in the back window. It's not just opening mail that I had to deal with. I had to show up for work on time. I had to pay taxes. I had to get car insurance. It's hard to believe I spent ten years of my life in an irresponsible fog, just kind of feeling that if I ignored the demands they would go away, or I could plead ignorance. But the hard truth is the demands don't change, they just get bigger, more adult, and the consequences of neglect get worse until pretty soon everything comes crashing down. For me, it happened at the Internal Revenue Service office downtown, sitting across the desk from a slightly sexy pencil pusher who wasn't the least bit impressed with my monologue about having to navigate a linear universe from the cockpit of my right brain:

"I've never been much of a math person, you see. I prefer poetry. Do you read poetry? I like Dylan Thomas quite a bit, but you look like a romantic to me, Byron and all that jazz."

The lady leaned back in her chair, crossed her legs, and spoke monotone without emotion. "You owe us seventeen thousand, three hundred dollars and ninety-three cents," she said, tilting her head slowly to the side as if she had delivered a line of verse.

"Shakespeare?" I questioned, jokingly.

"Uncle Sam," she said without a smile.

I don't think I turned her on. In the end, women are really attracted to guys who have their crap together. I doubt there are many women enamored by the idea of living in a box under a bridge, sucking on a bouillon cube while her man reads Emerson. This is probably not what the old ovaries are pining for. The thing about being irresponsible is it's only cute till you are about twenty-two or so, then it becomes a liability. One day you wake up under a pizza box, the television blaring in your bedroom, the laundry piled up over what might be a bedside table, and you ask yourself: *How did my life get like this? Why don't people like me? Didn't I have a cat and what is that smell?*

———————————

I WAS LOOKING at the paper today, the cover of the *Portland Tribune*, and they posted thirty mug shots on the front page. There is a big controversy in town about folks getting let out of jail because the city doesn't have enough money to keep them locked up. The whole city is in an uproar—you wouldn't believe it. So I was drinking coffee and staring at these guys, some of them looking like me a few years ago, about twenty-five years old or so, not convict-looking, pretty normal, and if you read what they were in jail for, I could see myself doing the same stupid stuff back in the day. A few of them were driving drunk, a couple got into fights in bars, some of them were caught carrying weapons. The normal criminal fare. And then I got to really seeing the guys, not just looking at them but seeing them. When you truly *see* a person, you start wondering what his life is like and where he grew up and how he got to be the person he has become. I wondered how much they hated being in the paper, because if I were in their shoes there would be some girl somewhere I had a crush on and I would want to disappear because I knew she would see my face. There are certain girls who are attracted to the criminal type, but I have never been attracted to those girls, so it wouldn't help me.

I'm not somebody who believes that people in prison are worse than I am just because they are in prison. It is true some of our character faults stem from social dynamics, not individual responsibility. What I mean is, the folks in prison or who've made messes of their lives have truly made bad decisions, but what if they have made bad decisions because nobody taught them how to make good decisions? I used to believe the idea that some people are born into great families and get their college paid for, and others are born into poverty and don't get such benefits in life—the rich get richer and the poor get poorer. And this is true, generally. But suppose what is also happening is that the successful get successful because they make good decisions and, far from being a genetic legacy, the art of making good decisions can be learned.

To say it another way, I don't think a guy who is a successful lawyer is that different from a guy in prison. We are all just flesh and bone, just tissue and chemicals. The main difference between the lawyer and somebody in prison is that somewhere along the line, the lawyer learned to make good decisions, open envelopes and pay car insurance and this sort of thing.

Eighty-five percent of people in prison grew up without a father.

Those of us who grew up without dads, who had mothers taxed by the burden of single parenting, weren't *in school* the day the whole *responsibility* lesson was taught. I don't think there is any other voodoo happening than that. That's the bad news. But before we start throwing bricks through the windows of the children of The Man, we should know that throwing bricks through the window of the children of The Man is a bad decision. It's really that simple. There are bad decisions and good decisions, and if a person makes a string of good decisions, and keeps that string going, he is probably going to be fine. And by that I mean he is probably not going to go to prison for much of anything. Just because we grew up without dads or life was hard coming up doesn't mean we have to be complete idiots for the rest of our lives. We can be just as successful as the next guy, as long as we learn a few things. When you think about it, people do it all the time—climb out of the ghetto or whatever, earn a good income, provide for a family, change the direction of their legacy.

The change started for me when I walked out of the IRS office. All of that was my responsibility, I realized. I had put my head in the sand and let life happen to me. I was like a basketball player sitting at center court reading a book, meanwhile the game was happening around me. Reality was happening around me, and reality didn't stop even though I was daydreaming.

But here is the other thing I realized that day. I realized the reason I was burying my head in the sand was not because I hated The Man. The reason I wasn't paying taxes is because I was convinced life was a game I was not invited to play. It has to do with all that belonging stuff I was talking about earlier. I didn't know I could play, and I didn't know I could succeed. I knew in the cognitive sense, the facts told me I could participate, and certainly the flesh on my skeleton testified to the idea I was alive. But I'm talking about a very deep realization, a realization that life had been given to me as a gift, a kind of challenge or a game, a bit of a battle, even, an adventure, and God himself might have been asking me to wake up and take charge.

Taking charge is really about making good decisions. For you and me, it is going to be difficult. Making good decisions is like learning a new language. Some people are born into French homes, and they can speak French fluently; and some are born into homes where wisdom rules, and they are going to have a much easier time making good decisions than we are. But we can learn.

My first step was all willpower, which never works. I decided I was going to get my life cleaned up. I bought a little day planner and wrote things in it like "wash the car" and "meet with somebody somewhere." I was writing these things because staring at the blank pages all the time made me feel like a loser. But it only took a week or two before I noticed I was right back where I started. I would neglect a fifty dollar payment toward my IRS debt, or I would mouth off at some jerk who rubbed me the wrong way. But that's when I met a man named Salome Thomas-El. Well, I didn't actually meet him; I saw him on television.

I was having trouble sleeping one evening, so I turned on

Charlie Rose, who was interviewing this guy Salome Thomas-El. He was a black middle school teacher in Philadelphia, and he had a presence that made you respect him, a soft way with big words and the kind of peace that comes to a man when he has found himself, learned to love himself, and operates for the world out of strength.

Salome had started a chess club in his school, recruiting from the projects around the small campus. He told Charlie Rose what he wanted to teach these students was not how to play chess, necessarily, because chess doesn't really mean anything in the real world, but rather the art of making good decisions. He would walk up to kids hanging around outside a convenience store and ask them if they wanted to learn to play chess. Of course the kids said no, chess not being the most fashionable sport on the playground. So Salome would tell them that saying no to him was a *bad* decision, that if somebody offers to teach you something, you should give that person respect and ask more questions to find out if you might need this information in the future. *"That was a bad decision,"* Salome said to the kids, *"to dismiss me in that way."* The kids didn't really know what to say, so they got tough, threatening him. *"Ah,"* Salome would say, *"another bad decision. I can see that, if you and I were playing chess right now, you would be losing, because in chess, you cannot make bad decisions and win. You have to make good decisions."*

"Have any of you ever played chess?" Salome asked.

"I know how to play chess." One of the kids answered.

"What is the legal move for a rook?" Salome asked the boy. The boy stood there silently until finally Salome spoke into his shifting eyes, "You are telling a lie, aren't you? You do not know how to play chess. A lie is another bad decision. If you knew how to play chess, you would not make so many bad decisions. You would know, intrinsically, that the way to get ahead in life is to make good decisions. And so I will ask you again, and I want you to think about it for five seconds before you answer me. Don't answer right away, because this isn't wise. I want you to think about what I'm going to ask you . . .

"Do you want me to teach you how to play chess?"

The children stood there, confused but interested, until one of them blurted out nervously, "Yes, I want to learn chess."

"Fine then. You have made a good decision. This is the first rule of chess. Make good decisions. The only possible way you can lose in chess, and for that matter in life itself, is to make bad decisions. If you do not make bad decisions, you will not lose in chess, or in life. And the more good decisions you make, the better your life will be. It is as easy as that. Who else would like to learn to play chess?" And of course, the kids belonged to Salome from then on, and he has influenced hundreds of children, lined up facing each other, their chess sets placed atop long tables, their hands quick to punch the timers, eight-year-olds, ten-year-olds, teenagers, playing men five times their age and beating them. As Charlie Rose continued the interview, you realized that Salome Thomas-El's students are among the greatest chess players in Philadelphia, and they are going off to college, becoming successful, starting families, and raising children who feel secure in their homes. These are not the sons of doctors and lawyers, they are kids without fathers. But they learned what their father should have taught them. They've learned to make good decisions.

To me it sounded wonderful, that good decisions, that success or whatever you want to call it was simply about looking at everything like a chess game, that is, you could make good decisions if you wanted—it wasn't about fate. Listening to Thomas-El, I knew I could learn to make good decisions the way a person learns to play the banjo. I sat there and watched the interview, and I believed him. I believed if I made better decisions, I could stay out of trouble, and maybe even build a little life.

After that my friend Curt and I started getting together at this coffee shop to actually play chess. It was just a coincidence that had nothing to do with that interview with Salome, but I was amazed at how much I learned about life from playing the game. We'd play for about two hours, about three games or something, and we did so nearly every day for more than a year, and even though I never actually met Thomas-El and even though he never taught me all the life lessons he teaches the kids in his chess club, lessons came all the same. I actually started applying some of the basics of chess to the basics of life.

Here's what I mean. There was a series of lessons I learned

about chess that improved my chances of winning. For example, when I first started, I would line the pieces up, then start making random moves. I rarely lasted more than twenty minutes. But with each lesson, the length of my games increased until eventually I started winning. The first lesson involved having a strategy. Believe it or not, the first fifty times I played, I didn't have a strategy going into the game. And of course I always lost. Curt taught me a few opening moves that would not leave important pieces vulnerable and would set up attacks at the same time. Once I learned these moves, I would move the pieces, not just randomly or in a way that felt wise in the moment, but in line with a kind of overall plan. Now I realize all of this sounds trivial, but this became an important lesson for me in life. It had been a long time since I had sat down and set some goals, really got a vision for what I wanted my life to look like. I wondered if something so simple as spending an hour going through some goals and writing them down in a book could have the same effect in life that it did in chess.

This was about the time my dreams became more passionate about being a published writer. I had been working for a publishing company for a while and began to wonder, seriously, if it was time to make a go at a book of my own. So I sat down and made a list of some things I would need to do in order to get published. I needed a few chapters, I needed an editor I could send the chapters to in order to get feedback, and I needed a list of publishers I could send the book to. So I wrote all of this down, which took about ten minutes, then I decided I was going to do it, that this was my strategy for doing what I really wanted to do with my life. And amazingly, I did it. After writing it down, it just felt like this to–do list is what I was supposed to do with my time. I was supposed to get this list of things done. There wasn't any discipline involved, either. I had written down the plan, so my mind just assumed getting the things on this list done was what it was supposed to do.

I was kind of amazed at how much of my time I had spent wandering around, not really knowing what I was doing or where I was going, only wanting random things in a random universe. I don't know how many months, how many years I spent sitting and watching television, complaining to myself about how boring life was.

It wasn't long after this that I was looking at my first book contract. I smelled it, laid it on the floor and rolled around on it, took it to various coffee shops and set it on the table, hoping people would ask me what sort of legal thing I was looking at. I dropped it on the floor at the grocery store, asking people to excuse me as I picked up my book contract, that sort of thing. It was great. And I don't mean to make it sound like if you sit down and make some goals you are going to get everything you want in life, but I do believe if you don't come up with some kind of strategy you probably never will.

So, I started wondering if there really was something to this *chess teaches boys about life* thing, and I tried to come up with a few more lessons. I think some of them are pretty good.

The second thing I learned had to do with patience. Curt would beat me about half the time because he was very good, but I noticed the times I beat him were the times I didn't rush into anything. That's the thing when you're playing chess—you always see this terrific move, and then you make the move only to find you opened up a world of trouble for yourself. I had to take my time, think things through. I started looking at decisions like paths in the road, wondering where each path was going to take me. I learned not to trust my instincts, seeing that often something that looked like a good move would cost me everything. Sometimes I would even walk away from the table, go to the bathroom or just stretch and rest my head for a second. This annoyed Curt to no end, but if I took my time and didn't react, the percentage chance of me winning increased. On nights when I was patient, I almost always won. But on nights when Curt took more time, of course, he would win.

It sounds too easy, perhaps, you just get up and do some deep knee bends every once in a while and you win, but it isn't that simple. The most difficult temptation, in chess and in life, is the temptation to react. Reacting without thinking never, ever works. As boring as chess sounds, you'd be amazed at how much emotion gets pumping when somebody takes one of your major pieces. On the outside, you're

sitting there like an old man, but on the inside you're jump-
ing across the table beating your opponent over the head
with a Starbucks thermos.

So that's where patience comes in. I was tempted to react
by killing any of my opponent's pieces I could, but those are
never good moves. As far as I can tell, the trick is to stick
with your strategy, no matter what your emotions are telling
you to do. I mean, if a person can do that, he is going to do
very well in life, no matter what setbacks he encounters.

I realized I spent much of my time reacting. If somebody
offended me, I was quick to react rather than consider what
reacting was going to cost me and whether the price was too
much to pay to get revenge. I've found if a guy can control
his emotions, he is going to go a great deal further in life.
Sometimes that means walking away. And so even in casual
conversation with friends, I started being more calculating
about what I said and did, being careful not to offend, and
if offended, working to bring peace into the situation. The
trick is to stick with the plan. If the plan is to finish school
and become a doctor or work hard and move up the company ladder, then throwing somebody through a window
would be a departure from the plan.

I used to know this guy named Ben who was always
being chosen to lead everything. To be honest, the guy
bothered me for the longest time. We'd have coffee and I
would ask him a question, kind of enter into debate about
some stupid issue, and he would sit there thinking about it
then come back with a safe answer, very objective. Like I

said, it was annoying. But pretty soon I started noticing most of the guys in our circle respected Ben, really wanted his opinion about things, and the girls all wanted to date him. I realized, also, that what bugged me about him not entering into debate was that I wanted him to stoop to my level, I wanted him to be a reactor. The more patient and calculated Ben was, the more he was asked to lead and the more respect he got from everybody around him.

And so I started noticing the guys who weren't respected much in life—that is they weren't close to a group of guys, and girls generally felt uncomfortable around them. They were guys who reacted. They were too loud. They didn't control their body movements. They didn't sound wise when they talked. They would say whatever came into their minds before processing their remarks, filtering them, really thinking about where their comments were going.

I had to swallow my pride on this one. I had to act more like Ben. It took a lot of practice, to tell you the truth. I have this annoying character flaw in that I always want to be right. Somebody would say something that I disagreed with, and I would open my big mouth and try to correct them or just make myself sound smart. But people who react never sound smart. It's the people who don't talk who sound smart, the people who don't use a lot of words.

I think there are usually a couple languages being used when two people are having a conversation. The first is whatever words are being spoken, and they say whatever they say. But the other is this hidden language, the emotions that go pumping through a person, trying to get him to do and say things that are going to make him look like an idiot. I might say with my mouth something really wise and practical. But if I was just reacting, that other language would say I wasn't in control, I was weak, insecure. And that's the thing with Ben: he never looked that way. He always came off as thoughtful and reflective and in command of his thoughts and actions. It's no wonder he was always asked to lead.

I'm not saying we should all become politicians. That would be an aggravating universe, to say the least. But I know life got a bit better when I stopped reacting all the time. Because of this, I don't have a bunch of people mad at me.

I heard somebody say that a good idea was to count to five before responding to a threatening situation. At first I thought this might get confusing, as though we might be tempted to answer every question by whispering the number six but what this person was really doing was teaching people not to react. For me, five was a pretty low number. If we were just talking about baseball or something, that was fine, but if emotions got heated, I would have to count to a million. I would have to politely leave—tell my body to smile and say thanks or whatever, keep on counting, then go home and feel a lot of anger or bitterness or jealousy. But it got easier. After a while, you realize that by walking away, by not getting angry, you are winning, moving ahead, and you get addicted to it. You get used to acting wisely and you like it. You realize this is a better system because it offers you something. It offers you life.

———■———

BUT I'M LEADING you on. I'm making you believe wisdom is a sure thing. But that isn't true. Wisdom only increases your chances of success. The truth is we aren't always going to win. Life throws stuff at us we can't beat. It happens to everyone. The hardest lesson is learning how to lose. The thing about chess, and about life too, is we are all going to fail. Even if you win a game of chess, it's usually a bloody mess by the end. It stinks in the middle of it, because you lose one piece and you start thinking the game is over. I mean you really feel it. Your mind gets all dark and you start believing you are a loser, and you feel like quitting. You wonder how you got yourself into this mess, and your clouded judgment can't see a way out. I've lost a lot of chess games well before a game was over. I start seeing myself losing, imagining myself losing. But I noticed one time that, even after I had lost a major piece, I somehow managed to win the game. In a way, that game broke a trend. And the next time I got myself into that situation, I wondered if there was still a chance, and so I stayed in the game. I stayed with a strategy and took my time and well, I won more games that way.

It happens in life, too. I can't list the number of times I thought life was completely over, that I had ruined everything and was going to end up living in a box under a bridge. There was the Christmas morning, when I was a kid, I shot out the rear window of my neighbor's truck with my new BB gun, the time I spilled a half gallon of red paint on the new living room carpet, the time I stepped on my first girlfriend's pet turtle. Those were awful days, to be sure, but looking back I'm slightly amused that I thought I had ruined everything. It was just paint, just glass, just, um, a turtle.

Sometimes I wish I could go back in time, sit down with myself and explain that things were going to be okay, that everybody loses ground sometimes and it doesn't mean anything. It's the way life works. This is hard to understand in the moment. You get to thinking about the girl who rejected you, the job you got fired from, the test you failed, and you lose sight of the big picture—the fact that life has a beautiful way of remaking itself every few weeks. The things that matter right now aren't going to matter a month from now, a year from now.

I believe there is something called wisdom. John Mac-Murray would point me to the Book of Proverbs, which contains the brief Polaroid snapshots of Solomon, one of the wisest men who ever lived. They're just short little sayings, like the ones you crack open in fortune cookies, and they can be found right around the middle of your Bible. I wanted to start making good decisions, and I overheard John saying to somebody this was a good place to start for basic life wisdom. I started reading a chapter every morning or every evening before I went to bed. You wouldn't believe how often the verses come back to you when you are just doing everyday things. I think if you read Proverbs, or the Bible in general, your percentage chance of success goes through the roof. Two thousand years of tested wisdom can't steer you wrong. If you really want to learn to make better decisions, the book of Proverbs is a good place to start.

Like I said, none of us is going to get it perfect, but you have to figure, a guy who goes into his life with a bit of strategy and a whole lot of patience and doesn't give up when he fails is going to be fine. It works for Salome Thomas-El's kids, and I think it will work for us too.

9

Friendship

You Become Like the People You Hang Out With

L ast month I visited a prison in Texas. I had the chance to guest-teach a class in a progressive rehabilitation program. I taught, but mostly I listened. As the guys told me their stories, their reasons for being in prison, I noticed a common thread. The real reason they were in prison was not because they had committed crimes, though they had, but rather it was because of the people they hung out with. Almost all problems and success in life boil down to relationships. These guys had gotten themselves into relationships that led to trouble. Either they had joined gangs or hung out with drug addicts or met girls who took them down a bad path. The reason they were in prison was because their friends, in a way, put them there.

I'm not saying they weren't responsible for their own actions, because they were, but I am saying that taking responsibility for their lives should have started a long time before they committed their crimes. It should have started when they chose to get involved with the friends they got involved with. We become like the people we hang out with.

Everybody needs love and affirmation, and there are appropriate ways to get it and inappropriate ways to get it. Because people like me—and some of you—grew up without both parents, there is a good chance some of that affirmation wasn't received. And so it might have made us a little desperate. I was a loud kid, I acted out, I got in trouble a great deal. I'd put on a show for people, trying to make them laugh. None of that is bad at all; in fact, that behavior, once matured, led to my current career as a writer and speaker. But early on it wasn't healthy. I was just trying to be noticed because I was designed to be noticed, and the people who were supposed to notice me weren't there.

And so when they didn't notice me, I acted out more. And got in more trouble. And honestly, I became annoying. I'd annoy adults, and they'd just stay clear of me or roll their eyes. And then I started feeling sorry for myself and acting out more. I was asking for attention and affirmation, but I wasn't asking for it in an appropriate way. It was a cycle, and it wasn't getting me anywhere. The people I wanted to be friends with at school wouldn't have anything to do with me, mainly because I was loud and annoying and I'd embarrass them, so I ended up feeling left out. I assumed I was being left out because I was some kind of victim, but the truth is I was being left out because, well, I was annoying.

I know there are all kinds of reasons people get left out. There's racism and prejudice and all of that. Not everybody who is left out is left out because of something they did. But that said, there is a lot we can do to assure ourselves we have good friends.

Like I said, we were designed to be affirmed and loved, and there are appropriate ways to ask for that affection. The primary way to receive the attention and affirmation we need is to affirm and care for others. I'm not talking about being sappy here. That would annoy people. I'm just talking about being a good, loyal friend. We think that people will like us more if we are funny or athletic or good looking, and some of that really does bring us attention, but what everybody really wants in a friend is somebody who is self-assured and loyal. I say self-assured because nobody wants a guy hanging out with them all the time who is kissing their butt. Don't beg for friends, just be a friend.

A few years ago, I handpicked some guys I wanted to be friends with. I already had some good friends, but knowing you become like the people you hang around, I decided I wanted to take more responsibility for who I was becoming. I looked around and identified about four guys who didn't know each other very well, but each of whom I wanted to be like in some way. They owned their own businesses, they were faithful to their wives, they were intelligent. I asked each of them if they would get together for breakfast on

Tuesday mornings in Portland. To my surprise, each of them said yes. And so we met. I told them that, essentially, I thought of them as great guys and wanted to figure out how we could spend more time together, helping each other's businesses and running our lives through the collective filter of our experiences. Amazingly, each of these guys had been looking for the same thing. It's something we all want, after all. The guys loved the idea, and for more than two years, we'd get together and talk at the same café on Tuesday mornings.

We didn't have much of an agenda, really, just to talk about life and to be honest. Months would go by, and I wasn't exactly sure what I or they were getting out of our time together. But looking back, I can see some of these guys have become close friends. I can see that I'm no longer lonely for brotherhood, or for that matter, for wisdom and accountability. One of us has since gotten married, and we are celebrating him and his bride. Another just had a son, and we are celebrating the creation of his family. In a way, I now have brothers to share life with, to do life with. And I am becoming like them too. These aren't guys who complain about their bosses or disrespect their wives. And so, naturally, when I encounter men who do that sort of thing, it strikes me as weak, and I pull away. That's just not who I am. Or rather, that's just not who I want to become.

All that to say, it might be time to look around at the people you're hanging around with. Are they the kinds of people you want to be like? I know that sounds terrible, like

I'm asking you to disrespect your friends. I'm not. But I am asking you to be honest. Are they holding you back? Are they really good friends, or are they just using you? Are you going to end up in jail if you keep hanging out with them, if you keep doing the things you are doing in order to get them to notice you or affirm you?

If you don't want to leave your friends, it might be time to have a hard conversation and explain you want to move on, maybe go to college or learn a skill. And you can invite them to join you. If they don't want to, you certainly gave them a chance.

If that doesn't work, you need to find a new community. It might be lonely for a while, but you've got to do it. Don't say you can't, because you can. Go online and find a kayaking class, a chess club, a book club, a karate class, an internship. Take responsibility for your life. If your friends are heading to prison, leave and head in the opposite direction. Find something better. The world needs you to be a better person.

10

Dating

How to Choose and Keep a Mate

On that same day I spent in prison, I was surprised at how many guys were in not because they were in gangs, but because they were led astray by a woman. When Solomon sat down to write Proverbs, an entire book devoted to giving young men wisdom, he spent more time talking about girls than anything else. He did this because, quite honestly, they matter more than anything else. A woman can make you a great man or she can destroy you. The trick is to find one who will help you become a great man—like Jack Nicolson said in *As Good As It Gets*: "You make me want to be a better man." It's true for both sexes. Nobody will mold you more than your spouse.

I actually met Michelle Obama once. We were backstage at the Democratic National Convention in Denver. I was there to deliver the closing prayer, and she was the keynote speaker. She and the girls came into the greenroom where I was seated. All the Secret Service were standing outside the door, the other speakers, handlers, along with a half dozen cops who traveled with her were standing at the door looking in. I had no idea why I was allowed to stay in that room, but I was. She walked in, very tall and dignified, wearing a beautiful dress. Her two girls were at her side as she came to me to shake my hand. I reached out my hand and greeted her, and she looked me in the eye and smiled. I knew she would be coming into the room, but honestly I never expected her to have such a presence. The woman is beautiful. She carries herself with a quiet dignity, a polite sophistication as though she could beat you at Scrabble but would spare you the humiliation. I knew when I met her she would be the first lady. I knew she would be the first lady even more than I knew her husband would be president.

People have always said it is the woman who makes the man, and I think they say this because it is largely true. Barack Obama was a radical success before he met his wife, but my guess is when he started dating her, he knew he better step up his game.

I only say all this because when it comes to choosing a mate, you'd best choose well. That woman or man will have more to do with who you become than any other force in your life. And they will influence who your children become too. This is not a decision to take lightly.

Before you figure out how to attract the opposite sex, it's

best to decide who you want to become. Once you know who you want to become, you'll better know who an appropriate mate will be. Have a really strong vision for what you want your life to look like. Are there other couples you know that you want to be like? How do they live? What are their mates like? Keep that in your mind and try not to settle for anything less.

I'm not saying to be a jerk about it. Nobody is perfect, especially you. But I am saying you want to partner with somebody who matches your vision, and you don't want to settle for less. That said, though, at a young age we are hardly who we are going to be ten and twenty years from now. Unconditional love heals people, and even somebody who has all kinds of issues can become somebody great. The question is whether or not that person really wants to move on and get better. If they don't, you aren't compatible, and you should chose somebody who is heading toward your vision, or who at least has the strength to go with you.

We also have to understand why we are attracted to the opposite sex, and there are many reasons. I want to talk about the two dominant forces that draw you to the opposite sex. The first is the desire to reproduce. This is what your body wants. The second is the desire for redemption. This is what your soul wants.

At a young age, your hormones are going crazy. We think we are in love but the truth is, we are in lust. We just want to have sex. But look around, look at how many couples are unhappy. So many of them got married because they wanted to have sex, not because they really wanted the responsibility of taking care of another person and a family.

The other force is the desire for redemption. Psychologists theorize that we are deeply attracted (what feels like romantic love) to the negative characteristics of our primary caretakers. You know that intense feeling you get when you think you can't live without him or her? What you are really feeling, according to some psychologists, is the desire to go back in time to when you were a baby and fix the relationship you had with your parents. That's why you feel like you've *always known* this person or that if you don't have him or her, you won't have any security. You feel that because your subconscious brain thinks that person is your mommy or daddy. Your squirrel brain is picking up on the negative characteristics of your primary caretakers because those are the ones you hope to fix. If your father had a bad temper, you might be attracted to a person with a bad temper. If your mother was controlling, you are going to be drawn to a more controlling person. And the whole time you are going to think you are madly in love, that this other person is going to complete you. They won't. The greater the passion, oftentimes, the greater the let down. This is true because the subconscious brain doesn't get what it was hoping to get, which is a repaired relationship with mommy and daddy.

Nuts, isn't it? Insane. But this is that theory, and I actually think it bears a lot of truth.

But what do you do with this?

Well, for starters, you don't let your squirrel brain drive all your decisions. When you fall in love, ask yourself what it is that is drawing you to this person. Is it sex? That won't last. It won't be long before you're sexually attracted to somebody else, and you'll just end up having many partners and the lonely life of a sailor on shore leave. Is it that they are controlling or have anger issues? That won't work either. They aren't your mommy or daddy, and they aren't going to make everything okay.

In fact, relationships, while rewarding, actually make life harder. They will bless your life, but they will bless your life through sacrifice. You are going to get more muscle out of it, and that's the attitude you have to have going into it in the first place.

So the real question to ask is "Can I put up with this person?" That sounds awful, but it's important. Does she like what I like, is he easy to talk to, is she a good friend? Of course, you have to be attracted to the person, just don't let that attraction hijack you into making stupid decisions.

That narrows the field considerably. You might be ticked at me right now because it's hard enough to get a date, and I've just taken ninety percent of the applicants out of the picture. But I promise you, people who know what they want and are choosy about their mates are infinitely more attractive to the opposite sex.

I wish somebody would have told me that when I was a kid. Because I grew up without a dad, I had no idea what women were attracted to. I never saw how a man interacts with a woman, and so it was always a mystery as to why my friends could date so easily and I was scared to death. I made a fool of myself, basically begging for love. It never worked.

———■———

I'LL TALK A little about what men need in women in a minute, but first I want to talk about what girls are looking for in a guy. Every girl is different, but what I learned over a long period of time was that women are essentially attracted to confidence and mystery. I don't mean to sound like a guy who is helping you pick up chicks. Please don't think that. But I want to save some of you from floundering around.

Girls don't want a weak guy. People are insecure already, so they don't want you to be insecure. Intuitively, they know they have eggs inside them that, eventually, are going to become little children, and they are looking for a mate who can provide for them and their eggs. If you go begging for love, they intuit that something is wrong, something is weak, and you won't be able to take care of their eggs. Instead, you are just acting like another egg that they are going to have to nurture. And if they do like you, they have their own issues and you don't want any part of it. You don't need another mommy. You need a wife.

What I am not saying, though, is that you should *act* confident. Don't *act* confident, *be* confident. And you can't be confident by looking in a mirror and telling yourself you are confident. Take a break from dating for a while. Seriously, you have other work to do. Instead, take up a hobby and get good at it. Start playing the guitar or a sport. Get good at something and improve your self-esteem. Once you've gained confidence, you can start thinking about a woman.

And they also like mystery. But it's not really mystery that they like, it's strength. Girls don't want you calling them all the time. They don't want to be your rescuer. If you call them all the time or let them know you are thinking about them all the time, you are going to turn them off. The truth is, you should already have a full life you are invested in, and you should invite them into that life. My friend John Eldredge says you should be on an adventure, and you should invite them into that adventure. A girl doesn't really want you to stare into her eyes like a lovesick puppy (at least not for long); she wants you to put your arms around her and stare into the horizon, to the place you are going to take her.

Here's another thing that it took me a long time to understand. And it's going to hurt. But I have to say it. *Human attraction is conditional.* Now, once you get married, you are committing to love your wife or husband unconditionally. But attraction remains conditional. Guys, if you get weak, your wife may stay with you, but chances are she's not going to be very attracted to you. Understanding what it is your mate is attracted to, be it strength or beauty, and giving that to them is a way of serving them. If you refuse to take responsibility for your life and expect your mate to still be attracted to you, it's going to be a long, hard journey. Self-pity is unattractive.

Weakness really isn't attractive in either sex. Some girls think being weak will attract a strong man, but it won't. Being weak will attract a predator, which is why girls who are full of self-pity always get hurt in the end. Bad guys smell it out and take advantage of them. The girl thinks he's strong because he's bad, because he's confident and mysterious, but really he's insecure and is only using her to make himself feel like a man. It's a cycle, though, because once a girl gets used, it gives her something to feel sorry for herself about, and she just starts all over, attracting predators.

If a girl wants a great guy, she has to stop feeling sorry for herself. She has to do something different to attract somebody different. A truly strong, hard-working man has no time for a victim. If you are strong and choosy, if you have a vision for your life, he will sense in you somebody to partner with so the two of you can help others. That's what he's looking for. I'm not saying you can't cry on his shoulder every once in a while—he will love taking care of you—I'm just saying if you lie around like a wounded animal, you are going to attract somebody who eats wounded animals. You aren't going to attract a knight in shiny armor.

Guy are attracted to beauty. But that doesn't mean you have to look like a supermodel. In the vision I have for my wife, she doesn't look like a model at all. She's going to be the mother of my children for heaven's sake, and she's going to have to entertain at parties, because God knows I don't want to make chit chat all night. So a girl throwing her boobs all over the place may get my attention, but she's not getting a ring. At least not from me. Beauty is important, but it's true there are many ways to be beautiful. I know good-looking girls get more attention, but most of them aren't any happier, and they are much more likely to get used. Guys treat them like celebrities, but what that girl really wants is to have a conversation. Self-assurance is beautiful. A choosy girl is beautiful. Intelligence is beautiful. A girl who isn't begging to be loved is beautiful. A woman who loves God is beautiful. A woman who does not manipulate men with her appearance is beautiful. God knows there are plenty of books out there for girls on how to attract guys. I'd be careful and read the ones from dignified, older authors, because there are all kinds of tricks women use to attract men that just leave them more and more lonely.

———■———

IN THE END, we have to understand that dealing with the opposite sex is very confusing, and you will be led astray. But when you are, ask yourself why, and for heaven's sake don't make the same mistake twice. Are you attracted to the negative characteristics of your primary caretakers? Are you filled with lust? Are you weak and attracting predators? Are you weak and turning girls off?

And here is worse news: We are not going to get the love

we really need from each other. We are going to get it from God, in heaven. Until then, we have an awesome opportunity to *practice* God's love with each other. We get to commit to each other, we get to try to love unconditionally (at which point we will understand how amazing God is), we get to serve each other by being more attractive to our mates, we get to take care of each other, we get to bring children into the world and take care of them, we get to share our lives with a family. And we get to improve our character. Those are the reasons we should be looking for a mate. Any other motive for getting into a relationship is going to let us down.

11

Sex

The Value of the Dollar in Argentina

A few weeks ago I was at the University of Texas. Some guys asked me to come to their fraternity house to have a talk, just a lot of us sitting around in the middle of the night. They wanted to talk about faith and morality. We left campus pretty late, weaving through side streets, past an outdoor bar spilling with students standing awkwardly next to each other, dressed for mating, cackling like birds. The fraternity house was a multimillion dollar limestone and cedar complex with a restaurant kitchen and dining area, ten-foot high fireplaces and leather chairs, couches sunk into a polished concrete pit surrounded by a gallery of black–and–white photographs: the watchful eye of fraternity fathers, fifties Longhorns holding football trophies, bottles of beer, their women standing behind them all

lipstick and teeth, hair pinned back like nurses at Pearl
Harbor.

"In the bathroom of this place there's a stack of porn with
Blue Like Jazz sitting on top," one of the guys said to me as I
walked in the house. The guy was the son of an oil tycoon, a
sort-of Christian. He said this not smiling, just stating a
fact, letting me know who I was about to talk to.

He led me through the dining area, through some heavy
double doors into the room with the pit of leather couches,
the young men already seated, quiet, fidgety, not sure they
wanted to be there or why, as though meeting to talk about
spirituality was akin to talking about *Star Trek*. They all got
up and shook my hand, about fifty of them. They leaned in
like their fathers taught them. They looked me in the eye—
glad you are here, good to see you, thanks for coming, liked
your book, glad to have you at Texas—all that.

"There's a bar full of women down the street," I said,
thumbing toward the window as I sat down.

"Dollar beer night," one of them nodded.

"Why aren't you there?" I asked.

"They do it every week," somebody said.

"So, you want to talk about faith, about God," I stated,
almost as a question. Nobody answered for a minute.

"It's not easy," one of them finally said.

"Being a Christian?" I asked.

"Right," he confirmed.

"Unless you live in the suburbs and surround yourself
with Christians who validate your identity, following Jesus

is going to be difficult. You haven't chosen to do that." As I said this, it seemed to let some of the stiff air out of the room.

"You think it's okay to live here?" another asked.

"I think it's wrong to run and hide. I don't know if it's right for you to live here. That is different for every person."

"There's not a lot of morality around here," one of the guys spoke up. "I mean it's a good-old-boy faith, you know. You're a Christian because every good Republican is a Christian. But . . ." This kid was fidgeting a bit; he slid down a little in his chair.

"But what?" I asked.

"But," he said, as a statement, shrugging his shoulders.

"But beer? But women?" I asked, finishing his comments.

"But women," another of them clarified, dismissing the beer as a minor problem.

"What is the thing with women around here?" I asked.

"It's difficult, you know. You're weak if you don't sleep around. The Mayberry act doesn't get you far."

"I see," I said.

"They're kind of everywhere. You've been around campus."

"I have. They are everywhere, that is for sure."

"Right," one of the guys on the couch leaned in. "And I really like them. I mean, you know, I really like it." When he said *it* some of the guys laughed. I nodded my head. "I'm not saying it's right," he continued. "I'm just saying, I like it. I like sex. Do you think I'm going to go to hell or something?"

"I don't think having sex is the way you get to hell. Heaven and hell are about who you know, not what you do. *Who you know saves you from what you did and who you are inside.* I'm not saying that gives us license to go have sex anytime we want with any woman we want. Morality is more important and more beneficial than any of us know. But heaven and hell are something different."

"It's wrong, though," one of the guys said, almost as a question.

"Yeah, I think it's wrong," I started in. "But let's not turn the idea of right and wrong into coloring book material. This is a very complex subject. Sin, if we want to call it sin, is stuff that we do that God doesn't like, and the reason he doesn't like it is because he loves us, he is fathering us, and when we sin, we weaken ourselves, we confuse ourselves, we practice immaturity. He doesn't like that, not because he wants to feel powerful or right, but because he wants what is best for us. That's the first thing we have to remember about all of this."

"Sex doesn't feel wrong," one of the guys said, leaning forward a bit, being slightly sarcastic but also honest.

"Okay," I said. "Let me explain it another way. You guys are all Republicans, right?" Most of the guys nodded their heads *yes*. "Well, let's consider the value of the dollar. Ultimately, logically, the dollar has no value at all. It's a piece of paper. It only has value because we say it has value and because we agree on a system of bartering that maintains that value. Great care is taken to keep the value of the dollar strong. Smart guys in Washington and New York lose sleep over this. And we all watched what happened in Argentina a few years ago. We watched what happened when the value of a currency declined rapidly. It's not a good thing. Sex is like that. God is concerned with the value of sex staying high. It's important to a person's health, a family's health, and a society's health. But like anything, sex can be cheapened in our minds, so we don't hold it in high esteem. God doesn't think this is a good thing. Stuff God doesn't think is good is called sin."

"What happens when sex is cheapened?" somebody asked.

"A lot happens. The main thing is there is no sacred physical territory associated with commitment. There can still be emotional territory, but there isn't anything physical, experiential, that a man and a woman have only with each other. Sleeping around does something to the heart, to the mind. It leaves less commodity to spend on a sacred mate. But all of that sounds pretty fluffy. Let me break it down into practical stuff. Women saying no to men, not letting men have sex with them, causes men to step up. If, in order to have sex with them, women demanded you got a job and shaved every day and didn't dress like a dork or sit around playing video games, then all of us would do just that. We all want to have sex, right?"

"Amen," one of the guys said, which drew some laughter.

"So if a woman demanded that you acted like a gentleman," I continued, "that you were able to commit and focus, then everybody in this room would do just that, if for no other reason than we want to have sex. And this in turn would be good for families, would be good for communities. Let's face it, we're guys, and too often we are going to take the path of least resistance. Many of us are the way we are because women are attracted to a certain kind of man. We may not have realized this dynamic was shaping us, but it has been. Nobody is exempt. So, when sex gets cheapened, we are getting what we want without having to pay for it. That's not good for anybody, not in the long run anyway. It's a great system, you know."

"But women don't withhold sex. It doesn't work like that any more," a guy from the back of the room stated.

"That's true," I said. "Women are imitating men, I think. The presupposition is that men are right, and in order for a woman to be successful, she should not act like a woman but like a man. Thanks for the compliment, but I disagree. I think men need women to be women, and we need to be made to jump through some hoops. If a woman withholds sex until she gets what *she* wants, we are all better for it."

There was some silence after I said this. Some of the guys were thinking about it, some of them I could tell were disagreeing.

"You know," I started in, softly, "I hate this as much as you guys do. You try to take away people's sex, try to make people feel guilty or something, and everybody hates you for it. I mean you're a geek, right? And I don't want to be that guy. I really don't. It's just that my dad left my mom when I was a kid, and I remember visiting him and he always had some girl living with him, or was sleeping around with a girl half his age, and that affected me. I think my dad just thought it didn't matter, that he should be able to sleep with whomever he wanted. But what I needed him to do was stay with my mom, love my mother, and be my father. I think we can think nobody is affected by our actions, by our habits, but they are. We aren't independent creatures, you know. We are all connected. And in a family, in marriage, it's important that sex be something special, and as men, it's important we take the initiative in protecting it. Those habits start now. Greg Spencer, a professor friend of mine, would say sex is the most psychologically involving of the physical acts. Men fantasize that sex is mere biology. Yet nothing seems to affect us quite as deeply as sex when it is abused. I hope you don't fault me for saying all of this."

"I think you make a good point," one of the guys said, crossing his legs and looking around the room at the rest of the guys. "But I think the thing all of us are dealing with is we are in this environment where we are going to be unfashionable unless we are routinely having sex and telling stories about it. Unless we are using women. That is the issue. And it's a powerful thing. None of us wants to be the guy who doesn't do that. I hear you, Don—" and he looked at me as he said this "—but the desire to not be marginalized may be stronger than the desire for sex. In other words, I would rather sleep around, get some pleasure, whatever, and not look bad in front of my brothers."

"Yeah, I understand," I said. "That's honest. Like I said, it's hard, you know, you are faced with certain challenges being a Christian in this environment. And you aren't always going to do well. But let's look at this another way. Let's say you had a friend who was forty years old, and let's say this guy played video games all night, slept around with ten different women, whoever he could get to have sex with him, drank all the time, partied it up, the whole bit. Would you respect that guy?" The group shook their heads no, some of them voicing that they would think of him as a loser.

"Why?" I asked. "Why would this guy be a loser?"

"Because he's forty," somebody spoke up.

"What does that have to do with it? If somebody in your fraternity lives like this, he's not a loser. Apparently, he is well-esteemed."

The group said that it was different because the other guy is supposed to be mature. He's supposed to have his life together.

"Yeah, I think so," I began. "I think he is supposed to be mature, because he is forty. But we've kind of said something here, haven't we? We've said maturity doesn't stay up all night playing video games and doesn't sleep with ten women. Maturity practices self-discipline and points a person's character toward a noble aim. And I think, even in your early twenties, there is this need for guys like us to grow up, to sort of usher other boys into manhood, into commitment, into self-respect and an understanding that actions matter to more people than just ourselves. Think of yourselves as prophets if you want. You're making a statement with the way you live your life. You're passing guys up, you are beating them to maturity. And there isn't any better way to help people than to have the boldness to pass them up. It makes them feel the pressure to mature themselves. I'm not saying this to be a wet blanket, you know. That's not what I mean. None of us has the right to judge our brothers. If you act mature, and don't judge others, you will be respected. I really think that is true."

The group and I talked till late into the night, talked more about sex, about spirituality, about the need for men, strong and good men, and how the world had emasculated us, turning us into thoughtless apes. Even as we talked I felt the things we were saying were true, that women need us to become strong, to be committed and control our desires for sex, and so doing, they affirmed exclusive unity, love, and family.

I won't lie to you. I've found myself wondering at times whether protecting the value of sex is all that important. Physical desire has a way of shaping a person's philosophy. But in the end I can't turn a blind eye to those who say that restraint is a good idea. It's true most people who make those statements don't make them well or winsomely, and they come off sounding anything but revolutionary, but underneath it all, the idea has merit. As a Christian, I know I need God to deliver me from a warped view of sex.

Not long ago I rented the movie *Kinsey,* a film about Dr.

Alfred Kinsey, a former professor of entomology and zool-
ogy at Indiana University. Kinsey caught fire when he created the Kinsey Institute for Research in Sex, Gender, and
Reproduction, which greatly increased the degree of honesty
with which people discussed their sexual tendencies and
habits. His research and finding is charged with the advent
of the sexual revolution in the sixties.

Kinsey's methodology mostly involved interviewing people in anonymity, using coding procedures so the greatest
honesty could be assured. His findings were mildly contro-
versial, setting the sexual instinct a bit more in the animal
category than conservatives felt comfortable admitting. As
his research continued, however, Kinsey's methodology grew
more compulsive until he encouraged his staff members to
have sex with each other's wives, and he himself seduced a
fellow male staff member. The thing became something of a
controlled orgy; and as the film depicts this slide, much of
the mental sobriety and focus of the characters gets dis-
torted. Staff workers were jealous of each other, wives felt
confused, Kinsey's research lacked point. In the end, Kinsey
realized sex cannot be removed from love, that the strictly
physical cannot be understood in isolation from the poetic
or romantic, that, in fact, animal behavior must be tem-
pered by morality stemming from something spiritual.

I thought of Kinsey's revelation again and wondered if
some of the more traditional views on sex could not, at least
to some degree, be supported by the very researcher the tra-
ditionalists have come to hate.

The great argument, then, is not whether sex is good or bad outside a relational commitment, but whether sex is *for* anything other than the release of pleasure. There is no scientific evidence to suggest sex is *for* bonding. Common sense tells us sex bonds people, but science can't go into the poetic. The tendency, when pleasure drives logic, is to reduce sex to a dry Darwinian definition, ignoring the poetry of our bodies. And this doesn't sound like much of a crime, until we remember the argument about the value of the dollar. Poetry, then, matters. What we feel about something, what we agree about for the sake of health and progress, becomes critical. I think of sex this way, not only because this is the way God thinks about sex, but because logically, even apart from some sort of Christian morality, the poetic interpretation has to be upheld.

12

—■—

Integrity

How to Pay for a Free Cell Phone

The first and foremost rule in the MacMurray home, and I've personally observed this, is *always tell the truth*. John says it's the basis for all healthy relationships. Trust can't exist without this rule working. Which reminds me of a story. John and I were sitting in the family room one night watching *Sports Center* when he asked about my new cell phone. I had set it down on the armrest, and he picked it up, wondering out loud at how small it was.

"I got it free," I told him.

"How did you get it for free?" he asked.

"Well, my other one broke, so I took it in to see if they could replace it. They had this new computer system at the Sprint store downtown, and they didn't have their records. They didn't know whether mine was still under warranty. It wasn't, I knew, because I had looked at the receipt before I brought it in. It was more than a year old. The guy asked me about it, and I told him I didn't know, but it was right around a year. Just a white lie, you know. Anyway, the phone was so messed up they replaced it with the newer model. So, I got a free phone."

John kept looking at the phone for a minute, then handed it back to me and went into the kitchen to get an apple. He came back and sat down, and we talked about the Seahawks for a while, wondering between ourselves if Holmgren could get them to the Superbowl.

"Did you ever see that movie *The Family Man* with Nicolas Cage?" John asked while taking a bite of his apple, leaving the conversation about football.

"I think I did see it, yeah. It's like Scrooge or something, right?" I asked.

"Something like that," John continued. "There's this scene in the movie where Nicolas Cage walks into a convenience store to get a cup of coffee or something, I don't remember. And Don Cheadle plays the guy working at the counter. Turns out there's a girl in line before Nicolas Cage, and she is buying something for ninety-nine cents, and she hands Cheadle a dollar. Cheadle takes nine dollars out of the till and counts it out to the girl, giving her way too much change, right?"

"Right," I say.

"And the girl doesn't correct him. She sees that he is handing her way too much money—change for a ten—yet she picks it up and puts it in her pocket without saying a word. And as she is walking out the door, Cheadle stops her, you know, to give her another chance. He asks her if there is anything else she needs. She shakes her head no and walks out."

"I see what you're getting at, John," I say, knowing he is trying to make me feel guilty about the phone.

"Let me finish," he says. "So Cheadle looks over at Nicolas Cage, and he says, 'Did you see that? She was willing to sell her character for nine dollars. Nine dollars.' " After John says this, he looks back at the television. He picks up the remote and turns up the volume. After a little while I speak up.

"Do you think that is what I'm doing?" I asked. "With the phone and all? Do you think I'm selling my character or something?" And to be honest, I said this with a smirk.

"I do," John said, not being judgmental, just stating a fact. "I don't mean to be a holy roller, Don," he continued, "but the Bible talks about having a calloused heart. That's when sin, after a period of time, has so deceived us we no longer care whether our thoughts and actions are right or wrong. And we have to guard against that. Our hearts will go there easily, and often over what looks like little things— little white lies. All I'm saying to you, as your friend, is, watch for this kind of thing."

"I see," I told him. We didn't talk about it after that. We talked more about the Seahawks, then about an old rerun of *The X-Files* that came on. John went to bed soon after that, and I surfed the channels and watched an interview with Richard Nixon from back in the day. He looked tired. This was after all the Watergate stuff. He looked tired but also relatively innocent. I'm not saying he didn't do anything wrong, I just mean by today's standards, he looked innocent. Basically, he cheated to get ahead in politics. That's hardly a crime today. It's almost like people don't even respect a politician who can't get away with distorting the truth. I didn't like that he looked so innocent. And I wondered why he didn't just admit he did something wrong. I went back to the Sprint store the next day. It cost me more than nine dollars, but I got my character back.

13

Work Ethic

How the Japanese Do War

During the years I lived with the MacMurrays, I discovered that children are loud. In the mornings they rise with the sun and get into the cereal before their parents wake. Within ten minutes, one of them has stabbed the other with a fork, and so you rouse each morning to the sounds of murder. If you place a pillow over your head or keep a fan running, you can ignore it for ten minutes or so, but sooner or later you have to go downstairs to lock the screaming one in the pantry.

When Chris was three or so, and Elle was a year and a half, both of them would get up early as farmers, even though they didn't have jobs. I slept late because after you see the sun rise over Mount Hood a couple times, you get over it and realize you don't have to *see* something beautiful to make it beautiful. It's beautiful whether you see it or not. So, after experiencing the morning ritual a few times, I decided to go back to my old ways of sleeping. The morning sacrament was a nice place to visit, but dreamland is where I belonged.

I say this because there aren't many pleasures I enjoy more than sleep. I sleep till I'm done, normally, and haven't set an alarm in years. I'm not lazy, mind you, I just find it odd that anybody would program a machine to wake them. God made the brain so it would wake on its own, and as a follower of Jesus, I'm a strict adherent to his system. Call me a fundamentalist if you want.

The awful truth about living with a family, however, is you don't get a lot of sleep. Unless you can afford a nanny or send your toddler to military school, which is what I intend to do, you are going to get up with the sun. There is nothing you can do about it. I tried to get around this fact, but after discovering I was using white noise and pillows to ignore the chaos of morning, Chris decided to start climbing the stairs to wake me in person. He would stand at the foot of my bed and stare at me, making me feel I was some kind of animal living in his house. I would tell him the guilt wasn't working, that I was a grown man and could sleep as long as I wanted, but he would continue staring, using all sorts of four-year-old silent tactics he probably learned from a book about how the Japanese do war.

"What do you want, Chris?" I would say into my pillow, my breath smelling like a litterbox.

"You sleeping?" Chris would ask, pulling his thumb out of his mouth.

"I'm sleeping. When Don lies down and doesn't move, he is sleeping."

"Dad says you sleep all the time and never stop."

"But I'm not sleeping anymore, am I, Chris?"

And about this time Elle, who was slow when it came to climbing stairs, would summit the top step to laugh and gasp, then roll onto my bed to poke her finger in my ear before she and Chris would jump on my head. Something else they probably learned from the Samurai.

I would push them off, but they would come again and no amount of pushing or kicking could get them to leave. I tried everything. I faked my death, gasping as though I couldn't get air, rolling off the bed, mumbling about being allergic to children. I slept in various Halloween costumes—ghosts, axe murderers, Raggedy Andy. But nothing worked. They would come, morning after morning, consistent and unfailing, like little droplets of water dripping on my forehead.

After twenty minutes of this, Chris would get bored or hungry and leave. This was hardly a relief, however, as Elle had yet to develop the courage to navigate the *down* direction of the stairs. She would stand at the top of the steps, face my direction, and let out the sort of scream a small town could employ to warn people of tornados. One found it hard to believe that such a small creature (four appendages and a head coming out of a pudgy diaper) could make such a loud noise.

"Scoot down on your butt, Elle," I would say into my mattress, my lips hardly parting under the weight of my own head. And in response she would warn me of tornados.

"Roll! Grip a pillow and roll," I would say, offering her one of my pillows.

She would gasp, cry again, all the while big crystal tears dove from her plump red cheeks, her arms outstretched in a request for me to carry her, the whole girl routine happening in miniature.

"Elbow. It's nine in the morning, for crying out loud. And a Thursday. Nobody gets up this early on a Thursday." She would stop screaming then, only panting, trying to find a breath through the hiccup-like convulsions of two-year-old lungs. And with this I would crawl out of bed, lean down to pick her up, and take her down stairs and into the kitchen. After a few seconds, her panting would quiet to awkward breathing, and she would slip her head into my neck, and then wrap her tiny arms around my shoulders, and of course she had me.

That is the thing with kids, isn't it? I believe God made them small and cute so we wouldn't forget to feed them.

———■———

"THIS ONE GOT out of its cage," I said to Terri one morning, bringing Elle into the kitchen and setting her on the counter.

"Did you go see Uncle Don this morning, Elbow?" Terri asked, leaning in to kiss Elle on the forehead while stirring a bowl of egg yolks. Elle nodded her head to say yes, her tears still wet on her cheeks, her breathing still post-trauma.

"Did you wake him up like I told you to, Elle?" John commented, coming over from the table, setting the newspaper on the counter.

"So you're the one sending the kids up?" I asked, genuinely curious as to whether John was interrupting my religious freedom.

"Don, it's nine a.m. I just can't stand it. How can you sleep this late?" He asked, looking at his wife and shaking his head, as though to ask her for an agreement.

"I'm staying out of it," Terri said, still stirring her eggs.

"I'm telling you, Don," John started in. "Enjoy it. Enjoy it while you are young and single. Sooner or later, reality is going to hit you, man, and you won't be sleeping in till noon. That's for sure."

"I get work done," I defended.

"You're a writer, Don. That isn't work. And let's be honest. You write every few days. The rest of the time you goof off, right?" John was being half serious now. And I was taking it a little personally, if you want to know the truth.

"Writing is like that. It's creative work," I said to him. "You just can't write every day."

"Sure you can," he said. "I've written term papers, I know about writing. You can write if you're not in the mood to write. You're just letting your feelings take over. It's all just work."

———■———

ABOUT THIS TIME, John and I started hanging out a little more, going on trips to get photos of mountains and sunsets and other free entertainments. The thing is, John is a hard worker. When taking pictures, he gets up early and heads into the elements well before the sun. When you are a nature photographer, there are two windows of time when it's best to take photos: sunrise and sunset. So John, who is notorious for staying up till two in the morning, would often drag himself out of bed at four to drive a couple of hours to a trailhead, then hike a couple miles into the mountains to set up for a shot of light coming through trees or first light on mountains. And these were the easy trips. The hard trips had him getting on planes and flying for hours into the middle of nowhere, then hiking for days into a remote wilderness or having a helicopter drop him off on a mountain peak in New Zealand, all for the hope of some sunset light happening a certain way on a mountain lake or mist settling low on a valley floor or a cheetah eating a porcupine or whatever else nature does. And John would be quick to say nature photography is the easier of his jobs. Running a business, teaching classes, and keeping Terri attracted to him require even more attention than shooting sunsets.

What I'm saying is the guy worked hard, and because of this, I learned a bit about work ethic. I learned, for example, a person could enjoy working, rather than experience it as a punishment. John and I talked about it when I went with him to take a picture in the Columbia River Gorge.

We had hiked to the top of a smaller mountain to get a

view of Mount Adams, across the river. It had taken us a while to get there, and I was breathing pretty hard at the top. Once there, John looked out at the mountain then up at the sky and wondered out loud if the evening sun was going to break the clouds.

"It's a great view regardless," I said.

"But it's not worth taking a picture of. Not yet," John told me.

"What are you talking about? It's unbelievable, man."

"Don, there are a million shots like this. Anybody could hike up here on any day and take this shot. We're looking for something a little more exceptional."

"I see," I said, but inside I thought the picture would be fine regardless.

John pulled his twenty-pound tripod out of his backpack and set it up. Then he carefully pulled out his four-by-five camera. It's an old looking camera you might imagine a guy using in the forties, as though he should have had a big stick in his free hand that would burst in a flash of sparks as he clicked the shot. John unwrapped the camera from some towels and set it atop the tripod, screwing the bottom of the camera to the top of the legs. He looked through the large opening, watching the clouds to see if any light was going to shine through. I went around and looked into the opening and saw Mount Adams in the distance, upside down in the sight of the camera, and the wide Columbia River wandering east, out toward farmland where it would eventually turn north toward Canada. I sat on a rock and watched the stretched-cotton clouds snag across the jagged spine of Mount Adams. I turned further north to see Mount St. Helens and then Mount Hood to the east and Jefferson directly south, and I watched as a boat in the distance worked up the Columbia toward Cascade Locks. And in all this silence and stillness and beauty, John began to unscrew the camera from the tripod. He wasn't going to take the picture.

"What are you doing?" I asked.

"The light isn't right," he said, setting the camera back into the towels and slipping it into the womb of his backpack.

"It's beautiful," I said.

"It is beautiful," he agreed, collapsing the tripod slowly, looking out at the mountain. "But it isn't right."

"Shoot it," I said. "We came all this way."

"We didn't come that far," he said. "And the light isn't right. I was hoping the sun would break through a little bit and put some color on the glaciers, but it isn't going to happen. High clouds are too thick tonight." And with that, he slid the tripod back into his backpack and loaded the weight onto his shoulders. "You want to look at it anymore or you want to head home?"

"We did come all this way," I said to him.

"I do have a family waiting for me back home," he reminded me.

"Okay," I said, putting my hands in my pockets and

turning to take one last look at each of the peaks. John laughed a knowing laugh at me under his breath.

"Getting it all in?" he asked.

"Well, I feel like we should have a moment of silence, you know. Something to respect the mountains."

"The mountains are piles of dirt, Don. Respect God."

"Well, maybe a moment of silence for God, then," I said to him.

"Fine." And John stood there for a second, kind of looking at the ground. Then he looked up at me and said, "You know, I do this all the time. I really love God and all, but why don't we head back home. God made my family, too."

"Right. Well, you've seen one mountain, you've seen them all," I stated, sarcastically.

"Exactly," John said, lowering a foot down the steep steps of the trail.

I took one last look at Adams, and let my eye glide upriver a bit, noting a waterfall happening in the distance on the northern shore. Then I turned and followed John down the trail. We didn't talk much on the hike back to the parking lot, but I do remember having a new respect for John, and I wondered how often it was that he made these hikes, sometimes ten miles or more, without getting a shot.

"How often does this happen?" I asked as we wound down the mountain in the truck.

"How often does what happen?"

"How often do you do all this work and not get a shot?"

"I don't know. I try not to think about it."

"Just guess," I persisted.

"It happens a great deal," he said. "I don't know, maybe I will use about 10 percent of the shots I take. Maybe a little more."

"Ninety percent of your work gets thrown away?" I asked rhetorically.

"Maybe less than that. I don't know."

"How do you do it, John? I mean how do you get out of bed at four in the morning or hike up into the mountains for days without knowing you are going to get a shot? Doesn't that drive you nuts, knowing the chances of your getting a good picture are so low?"

"But that isn't the way you are supposed to think about work, Don. It isn't about what you don't get done; it's about what you do get done. The price of one good shot is nine other hikes, nine other times I have to get out of bed. That's the cost of a great moment."

"You make pretty good money at this?" I asked.

"I make a lot of money, if that is what you are asking."

"How much money do you make?" I asked.

"None of your business," he said.

"A million?" I asked.

"What are you, my banker?" he chortled.

John continued to wind down the mountain, his headlights coming on to sweep through forest that seemed to grow denser the lower we descended.

"It's cool, you know. You get to do what you want and

make money at it. And a lot of money, too. How many people can say that?" I asked.

"It's a blessing," John said. "But you get to do what you want, too. You get to write books and all."

"Yeah, but I don't make any money at it."

"You think I always made money doing this? Ask Terri, Don. I ate a lot of peanut butter in the early years. In fact, for several years, we had very little. God *always* provided for our needs, but I remember when Terri and I were dating she would feed me dinner probably six out of seven nights. And if it weren't for her, I would never have seen a movie or gone out for a meal. She was always paying for our meals. It was more than a little humiliating. She was so cool though. She would never make me feel that way; only encourage me about what great photos I was getting. Terri has always had it together, man. I was just some dope with a camera."

"Terri bought you dinners when you were dating!" I said laughing to myself.

"Hey, that's how it is when you're trying to get started. It's the starving artist thing, you know."

"That's the cost of pursuing your dream, you mean."

"What are you, some kind of Hallmark card, now?" He laughed cynically.

"You're the one who lived off your woman," I said under my breath. We were quiet for a few minutes. Then, I confessed to John I didn't like to work. And I didn't understand why we had to.

"It's a crazy system," I started in. "God created us so we

had to eat and drink, and he created the earth so we have to work to get food and water, so that means God created us so we have to work. It kind of stinks. It's all about original sin or something, isn't it?"

"No," John stated, putting on his theologian hat. "It isn't. Adam and Eve had to work before the fall. Work isn't punishment; it's reward."

"How is it reward?" I asked.

"Well, that's the obvious question. And the answer is going to sound cheesy, but hear me out. It's about God," he said.

"God. So I should work because God wants me to work. So it's a guilt thing."

"No, not at all. Guilt should not be a motivation. Work exists for a lot of reasons. God worked. He created the earth and the cosmos. We work to participate in the God life, to imitate God. That's also why we take a Sabbath. Work is one of the ways we engage in life, one of the ways we participate. It's important. The Bible says that whatever we do, whatever work we do, we do it unto the Lord, to please him. Just like I do the things I know honor or please Terri."

"So, I get up in the morning and do work for God."

"Right. If you work for yourself, you are going to be let down, or you are going to work too much because you're trying to redeem yourself or something, or you are going to be lazy. God is the only motivation I have found where the law of diminishing returns doesn't apply. I get joy in knowing him, and he makes sense of my life, my family, my money, my work. And work is just a tool. It is the means to a good end, not the end itself."

"So, I could work a jackhammer, and it wouldn't matter."

"Working a jackhammer is a noble profession," John said. "That's the thing that gets to me, you know, because people think if they are somebody who does some kind of sexy work, they are more valuable. It's not true. All work is good work. Back in the day, do you know what I did?"

"What did you do?"

"I dug septic systems. I literally dug out people's crap and sucked it up into a tanker truck. And that is honorable."

"Sounds fun," I nodded with a smirk on my face.

"It wasn't. There wasn't anything fun about it, I assure you. But the work was honorable. It made me a better person. Nobody should be ashamed of the work they do. They should do it with pride and do it right. This guy I worked for, the septic guy, he prided himself in doing everything right. It was a great lesson for me. Have you seen somebody's lawn after they have had their septic tanks worked on or replaced? It's a mess, man. It is crazy, like somebody got buried back there. Not the guy I worked for. This guy had us scrape the grass off of the lawn, put it in the back of the truck, exactly like it was when it was on the lawn, then we dug out the septic, putting every shovel full of dirt in the truck so we wouldn't spill dirt all over the lawn, then we emptied the tank and ran a pipe down to the tank, so the next time we had to empty it we didn't have to chew up the lawn. Then we put the dirt back, but there is always too much dirt, because of the pipe, so we had to get a tamper out and tamp the dirt down so it would be level. Then we set the grass back on the dirt, exactly as it had been. I'm telling you, Don, nobody ever knew we were there. We did it perfectly. We would get calls every day from people wondering when we were going to be out, and we had to explain we had already been there, people on their cordless phones would argue with us, would yell at us to come and get it done, and we would have to prove to them we had been there. They couldn't believe it."

"That's crazy," I said.

"Yeah, but it is honorable. It taught me to take great pride in what I do, to offer people more than what they expect, to do work as unto the Lord. This guy was a Christian, the guy I worked for, and he told us that everything we do is an act of worship to God, even if it is, literally, sucking people's crap out of a tank in the ground. This was worship to him."

"I've never thought of it that way," I said.

"But do you see what I mean, about life being about God? When it is about God, it makes sense; it gives us a reason for doing what it is we do, beyond even feeding our families. It is bigger even than that."

"Work is worship," I repeated under my breath.

"Yeah," John confirmed. "So that means this: When I don't want to get out of bed to go and shoot this creation God made, that means there is a God problem in my life. It means I have to figure out what is going on between me and God that I need to deal with. Everything comes back to my relationship with God."

"You don't think of work as punishment at all?" I asked, wondering out loud if he really meant all this.

"Absolutely not," John said. "I mean, you can cheat or you can build something that doesn't honor God. That's different. But work, the idea of work, is God's invention, and it is part of our spirituality to do it."

14

Self-Pity

How to Annoy People and Be Downwardly Mobile

I have a friend who can't hold a job. He's actually had some great jobs, but he can't keep them. And for each job he's lost, he has a story about how bad his boss was, what an idiot he was, and how hard he was to work with. I'm sure my friend's bosses had some issues, but as I listened to him, I realized how hard it would be to have an employee like my friend, I mean to have to supervise a guy who was, at the start, against you, looking for faults, looking for reasons to not be a team player. Add to that, my friend won't take responsibility for his own issues. He assumes he doesn't have any. The truth is, my friend is destined to fail and continue failing, until he understands that what he really wants in life is to be a victim and that he's looking for any opportunity to become one. That's a cheap way of getting attention, and my friend will never be happy until he gives it up and starts taking responsibility for his life.

My friend Josh Ship is a speaker who goes around talking to large groups of teenagers. He is, perhaps, the greatest communicator I know. Even in my thirties, I watch all the little videos he puts out at www.heyjosh.com. Josh is an unlikely candidate to have become such a success. He grew up in more than twenty foster families. He never knew his mother or his father. That fundamental need we all have as humans to be loved and cared for. Josh never had filled. And yet he inspires millions.

I asked Josh once how he does it, how he remains so healthy. Josh said, "You either get bitter or you get better." It's that simple. You either take what has been dealt to you and allow it to make you a better person, or you allow it to tear you down. The choice does not belong to fate; it belongs to you.

There will always be a reason to feel sorry for ourselves. And sometimes it really is appropriate to grieve something terrible that has happened in our lives. But we also have to move on; we have to set ourselves free from the trap of self-pity.

If you are like me, the reason you sometimes feel sorry for yourself is because it feels good. I know that sounds odd, but if you think about it, it really does. When I feel sorry for myself, what I'm really saying is that I deserved better, that I am a better person than what the situation has dealt me. And if you think about it, that's kind of an arrogant thing to say. It would be better if our attitude was more like, *Man, that stinks, I didn't get that job,* or, *That girl rejected me; better luck next time.* Or we could just laugh about it with our friends. The trouble comes when something hard happens and we choose to stop and milk it for attention. There's no progress in that, and it isn't going to get us anywhere. And it's also annoying.

When people go to the gym to work out, they aren't building up their muscles, they are tearing them down. No kidding. When you lift weights, you are doing damage to your muscles. The reason your muscles grow, then, is because your body repairs the damaged muscles and makes them bigger so the next time you lift that much weight, you won't get hurt. So then you just lift more weights, and your body gets stronger and stronger.

It's like that with our emotions, too. Once we experience something hard, it tears us down. It really does hurt, doesn't it? We screw up and embarrass ourselves or we lose a job and don't have any money. But honestly, there is nothing bad that can happen to us that won't return a greater blessing if we let it. We will always come out stronger. And believe me, life is going to throw a lot of pain at you.

What self-pity does, though, is it stops us from gaining that emotional muscle. It's like God is saying, look, you can either have the blessing of a stronger character, or you can have the immediate gratification of self-pity. But you can't have both. People who wallow in self-pity never grow strong in character.

What we have to do instead is ask ourselves what we can learn from the situation. If we got rejected by the opposite sex, we have to ask ourselves why. Is there anything we can do differently? If we got fired, we have to take ownership of whatever we did that was wrong. And if it wasn't our fault, we have to understand that the rain falls on the good and the bad, and crops only grow out of ground that has been rained upon.

I have to check myself all the time for thoughts of self-pity. Now, I'd never consider myself somebody who feels sorry for himself. In fact, I detest the idea because I know how unattractive it is. And yet, nearly every day, I find myself complaining about something. And complaining is nothing but self-pity. If I complain about the flat tire on my truck, I'm really saying I'm somebody who deserves better. How arrogant of me, right? Instead, I need to get out of the truck and change the tire and move on, just dealing with the rain as it comes. Complaining is a form of self-pity. Another form of self-pity that creeps in is not wanting to do our work. If you don't like your job, quit and find a better job. But to complain is to not take responsibility for your life. You rarely hear powerful people complaining about their bosses. Why? Because people who complain about their bosses never become bosses. If you want to be successful some day, stop complaining. It won't be long before you are made the boss, I promise. And then you'll have to deal with all those people who are complaining about you. And that's a whole other topic.

15

Education

Jordan and Mindy's Dog

I grew up believing I was stupid. Nobody told me, but I knew. I say nobody told me, but my report cards said it, the red ink at the top of every page of homework said it, the frustration on my teachers' faces, all of this. Mom worked days and evenings when I was very young, so my sister and I came home from school to an empty house. We fed ourselves, and I walked the land on which we and several other families rented homes. There was a back pasture with a barn but no horses. There were barbed wire fences, and across the north fence was a field and across the field was a gas station with a store. You could get gum for a nickel. I never did any homework in the evening, and when my mother came home, tired and wanting to watch television, I would lie and tell her I had studied.

I had a terrible case of attention deficit disorder that made it hard to concentrate on anything for more than a few seconds. When listening to a teacher give a talk, I felt I was on a merry-go-round, hearing every fifth sentence. The rest of the time I wondered how dolphins talked under water or what a civilization of puppets would use as currency.

A person who believes he is stupid is worse than a person who is stupid. My friends Mindy and Jordan have a large dog who submits to a skinny cat. The dog is a pit bull, higher than my knee, muscle all down its back, hard to the touch on its breastplate. The cat shows bones and whines like a hobo. But the dog does as the cat suggests, because it does not know it is a dog; it does not believe it has any muscle.

All of this is about belief, I suppose because when you think you're stupid, you act stupid. My schoolwork consisted of getting by. Each year was about survival. I survived the day, the bully students, the teacher, my mother's inquiries. The idea that there was something more than survival never occurred to me. I did not know I could make good grades or that there was a world to learn about or such a joy as learning. Everybody was frustrated with me, and I felt the Ds and Fs were the bottom of boots kicking me into a hole, and I never thought I could come out, never thought I had the mind to claw and scrape. And so I rolled left when the boot came down and rolled right when it came down again.

More than 70 percent of students who drop out of school come from fatherless homes. This statistic from the National Principals Report a while back came as no surprise. With no father to ground the home, the mother works and is exhausted and is in no way free to nurture and support. I don't believe the sinful nature can be summed up easily, but I know part of it means a person left alone doesn't grow or get strong, not emotionally anyway, and certainly not academically. We all need to be pushed. I didn't get pushed a whole lot, not with the four hands of parents, anyway. God knows a teacher has her mind distracted, kids loud with profanity, and she doesn't feel affirmed by the student who just can't comprehend. And I don't mean to blame everybody else, because I was the one who didn't study and I was the one who didn't learn. But social conditions matter, otherwise fathers and teachers and mothers are of no consequence.

All that to say, the conditions were ripe to teach me I was stupid. And that was one of the few lessons I learned well. Grades, then, become labels. They could almost be considered price tags for my worth.

I never made anything above a C until my senior year in high school. Coming into my senior year, I didn't know whether I was going to graduate. My Spanish teacher allowed me into the twelfth grade on the condition I would never take another Spanish class again, for the rest of my life. It is a promise I've kept, but at the time, the condition offered no confidence that I could lean out across the finish line in subjects involving teachers less gracious.

I recall an evening when I was in high school, having failed another test, lying on my pillow watching the blades of my ceiling fan twirl and wondering whether or not I was mildly retarded. I know it almost sounds humorous, but it's true. That actually happened to me.

But all of this changed the second semester of my senior year. A girl I liked enrolled in a class called Honors Psychology. I went to the school guidance counselor to have my schedule changed.

"This class is only for students in the top ten percent," she said to me, lipstick on her teeth.

"I didn't know that," I told her. "And where am I?" I asked, glancing at the file on her desk.

"Well," she said, opening the file and pulling out my transcript, "you are not in the top ten percent. You are definitely in a percentage, but it isn't the top ten percent."

"What do I need to get into the top ten percent so I can take that class?" I asked.

"A time machine," she said, being completely serious.

"A time machine?" I asked.

"Right. You could use it to go back in time so you could start over and take school seriously." As she said this, she closed my folder and set it on her desk.

"You don't want to let me into that class, do you?" I asked.

"I can't. The class is for students in the top ten percent. I'm sorry about this."

"There is nothing you can do?" I asked again.

"Work on your grades, Don. There is no reason your senior year can't be great. Then you can make up for some of this in college."

"Right," I said, standing up and putting on my jacket. I stood in her doorway and wondered about something she had said. I rattled some loose change in my pocket.

"Can I help you with anything else?" she asked. I stood there for a few more seconds, not really talking.

"What is it, Don?" she asked, picking up my file and sliding it into the file cabinet.

"There's no such thing as a time machine, is there? You were kidding, right?" I asked, sort of looking at the ground. She paused, looking at me in shock.

"I was kidding, Don. Yes," she said, shaking her head in amazement.

"Right, then," I told her. "I knew you were kidding. So was I. Okay, nice talking to you. Have a nice day." And with that I walked out as quickly as possible. I walked across the hall, though, and made an appointment with the principal. He happened to be available right away and ushered me into his office.

"What can I help you with, Don?" he asked, a very big and friendly man with a model sailboat on his desk.

"I want to take Honors Psychology," I told him.

"But that class is for students in the top ten percent. You aren't there, are you?" He asked, wondering if he had my reputation mixed up with somebody else.

"No, I'm not. It's just that it's been hard, you know, to

study and all. I know I haven't done well. But for whatever reason, I want to take this class. Can you get me in?"

"Well, son, I like your ambition. I really do. But I don't think I can do that. It's a special class for special people, and it's not that you're not special, you are. You are very special—"

"Look, Mr. Martindale," I interrupted, "I would like nothing more than to have a time machine and go back in time to take school seriously. Because school is serious. Both you and I know that. But something you and I both also know is there is no such thing as a time machine. I'm smart enough to know that. And so are you. But I feel it, Mr. Martindale." I put my hand to my heart as I said this. "I feel it very deep. I love Honors Psychology. I ache for it. And if you could get me into that class, and perhaps get me a seat next to Nicole Locker, then you would be saying to the whole world there is always a second chance."

"I don't think the world is that interested, Mr. Miller." Mr. Martindale said. And then he did something that surprised me. He asked his secretary to bring him the student list for the class, and after inspecting it to find only ten students had signed up, he wrote my name on the list. To this day, I don't know why he did it. But I had never been so excited in my life. I was going to learn everything there was to know about Nicole Locker, and Honors Psychology too.

Mr. Higbee was the teacher. A former Methodist minister turned agnostic philosopher, he taught the class unlike any other class at the school. He taught it like a college class. We were asked to listen to lectures, weeks and weeks of lectures, and then we were tested. But we were not asked to regurgitate answers we had memorized; we were asked to think. We were asked to recall what we had learned and to expand, to write how we felt about it, what we agreed with and disagreed with. And to my surprise, after two weeks I had lost interest in the girl but gained an odd affection for dead personality theorists. Every two months when we were tested, I would write and write and write until Mr. Higbee would have to take the pen out of my hand and scoop up the pages from my desk. I was always the last student to leave. I loved the class. And to my amazement, indeed to the amazement of Mr. Higbee and Mr. Martindale, I finished with a 99 percent. Only the valedictorian beat my score.

It was this class that planted the seed of doubt that maybe I was not mildly retarded, but perhaps one of those special kids who can't speak very well but can play Mozart on the piano. Only I *could* talk, and my Mozart was stuff from a psychology textbook, only I didn't know it super well, just kind of well.

And although I realized later that year I was not autistic and had no hidden talents of any kind, I also realized, perhaps I was not stupid. And the seed of doubt about my assumed stupidity that started in Mr. Higbee's class gave way to another important realization. Back then, to wind down at night, I was in the habit of going on long walks around the neighborhood. And on a particular night it hit me, and it hit me like a meteor that had fallen from the sky: *I could be anything I wanted.* More specifically it occurred to me that I could be a lawyer, which is ridiculous because I could never be a lawyer, but the deeper truth persisted, and still does today, that there wasn't a glass ceiling above my head, that if I wanted to go out and make something of myself, I could. I know this all sounds silly and that most people realize this when they are children, but when you grow up hard, there is a part of you that believes life, college, a good job, money, all of this, is for somebody else, and you are not invited to that party.

I would love to say the struggle ended that night, but it didn't. It was a great night, but the going was still rough. Most of my friends went off to college, and because we didn't have any money, and because I hadn't applied myself in school, college didn't feel like an option. I know now that it was. I might have taken a few more years to graduate, but in the long run, this would hardly have set me back. At the time, it was difficult not to compare my life with the life of my friends, almost all of whom went off to school, lived in dorms, went to their college football games, and stayed up all night getting drunk at parties. But I lived at home, delivering Chinese food at night and taking classes in the morning, and I couldn't help feeling like a loser.

But that's when I learned about reading. I'm not proud of this, but it wasn't until I was twenty years old that I read my first book. I'm not kidding. I made it all the way through high school without reading much of anything, and certainly without reading anything cover to cover. But I had this friend, this pen pal who loved poetry, and for her birthday I went into a bookstore and got her a book of poems. The book was *Selected Poems & Letters of Emily Dickinson.* I'd never heard of the author before, but I thumbed through the poetry section at Barnes & Noble until I came across a female name. I flipped open the book and read a few lines, a letter the poet had written to her brother when she was only thirteen. And I was struck. I was struck at the beauty and muscle the young writer employed. She could pack more into a sentence than I could fit into a lifetime of rambling. I sat down in a chair and read half the book before finally getting up and paying for it. I wrote an inscription to my pen pal, wishing her a happy birthday, but I never sent her the book. Each day I would go to put it in an envelope but would read a few pages, then sit down to read the entire book again. I must have read the book fifty times. That pen pal and I became good friends, and after I moved to the Pacific Northwest, where she lived, she took "her" book off my shelf, claiming that though it was weathered and torn, it belonged to her, proving it by reading aloud the inscription I had written so many years before. I conceded and let her have the book, but got to missing it so much I broke into her house and stole it only a month later, and still have it on my shelf today.

I say this because something important happened to me when I read Emily Dickinson. I fell in love with books. Some people find beauty in music, some in painting and some in landscape, but I find it in words. By beauty, I mean the feeling you have suddenly glimpsed another world or looked into a portal that reveals a kind of magic or romance out of which the world has been constructed—a feeling there is something more than the mundane and a reason for our plodding. The portal is different for everyone. Many of my friends find it by studying physics or math, some from biology or music, but for me it has become literature.

As a by-product of reading, my vocabulary began to improve, and I was able to engage in conversations with friends who had attended school. I don't think there is any substitute for a college education, and I regret not attending myself, but a diligent commitment to reading will get you far. All leaders read, and there are almost no exceptions.

I moved to Oregon in my early twenties when a friend's father offered me a job in his publishing company. I intended to finish college in Oregon, but after securing the job in publishing, I realized I loved the work and was gaining more experience toward a career in books than I would at a university, so I put off school. One year gave way to another, and before long I was running the company and school seemed an afterthought. I'm grateful for my friend's father, because he trained me in a profession I love and am grateful to work within every day. But I also knew I had missed out on a liberal education.

That's when I discovered a person could audit classes at nearly any school in the country for a fraction of the cost of enrolling. I'm not recommending this as a substitute for gaining a degree, but if you want to keep learning, it's an option. I've taken classes on the humanities, on literature, on writing, and in theology. I think it's a good idea to take a class every year. Even though John MacMurray teaches at a local Bible college, for instance, he still audits theology classes, just to stay sharp. And I have another friend who created a "Doctorate of Jesus" degree in which he audited dozens of classes from several different universities in the Portland area. When he completes his self-created degree, he won't be able to get a job anywhere, but he will definitely know a lot about Jesus.

I don't think I'm stupid anymore. These days, I just think of the mind as a muscle, and by working it, we get more enjoyment out of life. I had a teacher in high school named Mr. Sleepak. He was our music instructor, and he used to tell us if we were coasting, we were moving downhill. He said this to get us to practice our instruments, but I think it's true in all of life. What I mean is, if we aren't learning, we are forgetting; if we aren't getting smart, we are becoming dull.

The latest statistic is that the average American watches 1,456 hours of television a year but only reads three books. So if it's true that readers are leaders, and the more you read the further you advance, then there isn't a lot of competition.

———————

BUT IN THE end, I have to tell you the truth. I don't think reading to get ahead is that great of an idea. It's okay, but it's not great. When I was younger, I didn't know *why* a person should read and commit to learning for a long time. It wasn't until I turned thirty that I understood—not till after I had some success, had achieved some goals, and realized they didn't mean much. It was then I understood *why* we should learn. I used to believe a person should read books so that when he or she runs for president, he or she would not sound like an idiot before the American people. But this isn't the reason we should educate ourselves, it turns out. I learned why we should learn from Annie Dillard's *Pilgrim at Tinker Creek*.

My friend Posie told me about the book and said she had to read it slowly, that she kept it in the top drawer of a desk and pulled it out like secret chocolate, reading a paragraph at a time, then slipping the book back into the desk to meditate. She spoke about the book as though it were an old lover. I told her I would buy a copy of my own, and she looked at me as though I were about to find faith. The book was indeed rich, and I suspect Posie read a mouthful at a time because the mind was not meant to digest so much so fast. Dillard wrote the book in her twenties and won the Pulitzer Prize for the effort. It's not a story, but reflections on the heavy surface of the earth: the life in a stream, arteries on a leaf, the wet shine of a turtle's shell coming out of blue-green water. The world falls away as the words combine, and the reader gains the peaceful frenzy of worship. Dillard loves life and wants to know everything. She learned the names of the flowers and the grasses, not because she wanted to run for president, but because the earth had reached up and grabbed her hand, pulling her low to press her palm against the breathing soil. I felt in reading her that we do not read books to learn, we do not learn to succeed; we learn because in doing so we experience something like the pleasure God felt in the act of creation. We discover his handiworks *with* him.

———■———

MY FRIEND GREGG used to teach teachers, and he states emphatically that students who are driven by delight will learn more than those driven by discipline. I take this to mean we should move to other subjects if we don't find ourselves enamored. Literature, theology, and psychology fascinate me, and so I consider the subjects a calling. This is my Tinker Creek. While I find a salamander boring, syntax stops my heart. And I wonder how many people think they are dumb when they are not, think academia is for others when it is for everyone. I wonder, when I meet a person who spends his or her life in front of a television, about the Tinker Creek they never discovered and where the creek might have taken them, to what heights, to what worship.

16

Pardon

Forgiving My Father

Yesterday I was visiting my friend David in Chicago. He's a tattoo artist with long black hair and tattoos that climb his arms. He looks like the lead singer of a metal band. To walk down the street with David is to have every fifth person look over and wonder if he is famous. He called and said to meet him at the Field Museum across from Soldier Field. He was there with his son, Xavier, who is four. Since the last time I'd seen my friend, he'd gotten a divorce, and we were getting together on one of his visiting days. I felt privileged he'd take the time to get together on a day he could spend exclusively with his son. I got out of the cab in front of the museum and spotted my friend and his son at the top of the enormous cascade of marble steps that falls in front of the building. David kneeled down to Xavier, pointing at me and waving, no doubt asking Xavier if he remembered me. Xavier is only four, and I'd not seen him for at least two years, maybe more. But Xavier later told me he remembered me from when he was a kid.

In the museum, David and Xavier walked hand in hand, and every experience Xavier had only mattered if shared with his father. Every elephant only became an elephant when Xavier pointed and told his father what it was. In David was all of Xavier's security, his sense of belonging, his identity. We spent a couple hours in the museum, and David told me the story of his year, the fighting with his wife, the fear of what the separation would do to his son, his genuine concern for his wife. I asked him if, when Xavier was with his mother, David missed him. We had left the museum by this point and were walking through a pedestrian tunnel that went back toward Michigan Avenue. Xavier had run ahead a little, to the other side of the tunnel, and David looked at me and said quietly that he cried himself to sleep every night. He said that when Xavier is with him, he sleeps in his bed, and without him he can't fall asleep. He said he just cries, and in the morning when he wakes up, he reaches over to feel if Xavier is in the bed with him. If he's not, David starts the morning crying, too.

It reminded me again of that bond that takes place between a father and a son. Or at least it reminded me of the bond that is supposed to take place.

The idea David would ever step out of Xavier's life is not a possibility. He loves his son. I thought again, though, about my father, about how I happened to get one of the guys who could just walk away without wanting to see me, and when David talked about reaching over to feel whether or not his son was there, I wondered whether my father had ever done that for me. But I knew in that instant he had not. The guy who reaches over to feel if his son is there, and cries when he is not, isn't the same guy who eventually walks away. I got a bum deal on a dad, there's no question.

Like I said, the last time I'd seen David was about two years before. I'd been in Chicago and had a couple tickets to a Bears game. David and I went, and I cheered for my Seahawks and David cheered for his Bears. The Bears won. It was on that same trip I met my father. In fact, it was the day before the football game. I'd been in Chicago on business and had recently discovered that my father was alive and living in Indiana. I'd not seen or heard from him in nearly thirty years. Through a friend, I'd gotten his phone number, and in fear and trembling I called him and asked if he'd like to get together. He gave me his address, and I typed it into my GPS and set out across Indiana to visit the man who never reached across and cried at his empty pillow.

I was nervous, obviously. My hand was shaking on the steering wheel. I didn't know why I wanted to see him, I only knew I had to. David was the one who encouraged me, actually. He'd tracked down his father the year before. His father had died, so he visited his grave and met his extended family, half brothers and sisters he'd never met before. David said the experience had given him closure. So maybe I was looking for closure. Or maybe I just wanted to live out a good story, something dramatic. I don't know. I only know I wanted to see my father and didn't want to see my father at the same time. These two desires were battling inside me as I drove.

I kept rehearsing what I wanted to say. In my mind I sounded like a politician, very formal with a handshake and all of that. And so that's who I was when I pulled up to his house. I got out of the car and before I could knock on the door, he came out. He was tall, a barrel-chested man who looked at me and told me in a deep voice that I looked great. He gave me a hug, invited me in, and I sat down on the couch. I don't know what I was feeling at the moment. I felt as awkward as a door-to-door salesman who'd come to sell him something, but I didn't know what I was trying to sell him. I felt like I needed him to agree with something and sign a piece of paper, but I didn't have a piece of paper for him to sign.

I don't know what he said at first. It took me several minutes to even be there, in the moment. The television was on some news station, and he didn't turn it off. He had a beer in his hand. He kept sipping from his beer, looking over at the television. But he talked. He didn't stop talking, in fact. That made me glad, because honestly, I didn't want to do any talking. I didn't have any questions for him, actually. I didn't really want to get to know him because I didn't want the responsibility of a relationship with him. I wasn't angry at him. It's not that I didn't like him, it's just that I didn't know him and didn't really want to know him. I didn't want to be friends.

But like I said, he talked. And as he talked I found myself liking him. He was charming. My mother warned me that he would be charming. I don't look like my father at all, but I sound like him. I mean his voice is older and deeper than mine, but the charm, I could pick up on the charm. It's the voice I use when I want to impress somebody. It's the voice I use when I'm talking to a good-looking girl. Even though I knew what my father was doing, I enjoyed it. Charm works, and his effort to be somebody I might like is actually a kind of compliment—at least he cared enough to be fake, you know. It's not like he was being indifferent.

My father told me the story of the divorce. He told me he still had feelings for another girl and that after my sister was born, he lost interest in my mom. He insisted he didn't want a divorce. He said when she brought him before the judge, he cried. He wanted to figure it out. But my mother had had enough. She wanted to go back to Texas to be with her family. My father signed the papers and that was it. But, my father explained, I followed her. I moved to Texas to be close to you and your sister, he said. I loved you, I really did. But the fighting continued, he said.

I don't remember my mother and father fighting, but I remember visiting him when I was a kid. And I remember the last time I saw him. He took my sister and me out to dinner. I hadn't seen him in about a year, and I remember always looking for a place to run if my father tried to kidnap us. I don't remember if my mother told me he might try to kidnap me or not, but that is what I thought was going to happen. As we drove to the restaurant, I kept an eye out for police cars, for apartment buildings I could run into yelling if I had to. Looking back, I know my father had no such intentions. He must have felt that the days of childlike innocence were over and that there was no more blind adoration to be had just because he was our father. I never saw him again after that.

But Dad said there was still fighting, and he said he couldn't take it anymore, so he left. He moved back to Indiana and got remarried. He'd been remarried for twenty years. I had a half brother I didn't know about.

I really loved you, he said to me nearly with tears in his eyes. Nearly, but not with *actual* tears in his eyes. He was being *kind of* sincere. I only know that because I can do the same thing. It's a form of self-deception, I think. I can feel genuinely sentimental about a situation, but not truly mean what I feel. I think that is what my father was feeling, sitting there with his beer and the television on the news.

But he apologized to me. He looked at me and told me he was sorry. He asked for my forgiveness, and I gave it to him. I told him I accepted his apology. And about an hour later, I got in my car and drove back to Chicago.

———————

AT THE TIME, I didn't know what forgiveness meant. I wouldn't really know what forgiveness meant for another year, until my pastor, Rick McKinley, happened to spell it out in a sermon. He said that when you forgive, you bear the burden somebody has given you without holding them accountable. Before I heard that definition, I wondered whether I'd actually forgiven my father. I didn't really want to see him after that. Or perhaps I did want to see him, but I didn't want to go through the emotional work it takes to rebuild a relationship that broken. And there is no way I trusted him. If I held something against him, it wasn't on the surface. I held it deep. So it all made me wonder whether I meant what I said, that I'd forgiven him. The way Rick defined it, though, meant that there was still pain, that we might still be paying the price for the wrong that was done to us. It's just that we weren't going to make the other person pay for what they'd done; we'd forgiven them. I thought that was meaningful and helpful, and that's what I decided to do with my father.

I'd love to have had a dad who taught me I was special, at least to him. I'd love to have had a dad like David, who ached to have me next to him. I still don't get how a father could be so selfish to walk away from his kids. There must be something missing in that guy's brain. We can certainly heal from these wounds, though. Everybody has something they have to deal with, and this burden is the one given to me—and some of you. But holding a grudge is just another burden. I had to let go and give my father a pardon. I had to no longer hold him accountable for what he did. I had to forgive.

17

---◼---

Empathy

Wounded Healers

What led me to spirituality wasn't only my desire to be fathered—although I like the fact that I am fathered by God. But what really lead me to spiritually was a desire to believe I was human and that being human mattered.

People have a problem understanding the value of being human. It's a universal struggle, I think. Even though I've highlighted the battles of the fatherless, I don't want you to believe that because you grew up fatherless you are alone in a world of well-adjusted people; nothing like this is true. If you sit down with your friends to scratch the skin, you'll find they have the same blood as you, the same decaying bone, the same issues, the girl issues, the athlete issues, the spoiled-brat issues, there's a whole catalog of issues available to us.

Sometimes a human life can seem no more meaningful than a fish flopping on a shore. Writhing. Out of its element. And I would love to tell you that the real problem in life is we *believe* we are writhing when we aren't, but that's not true. My spirituality, that is Christian spirituality, doesn't tell me to close my eyes and pretend life is beautiful and there are no problems to confront. I'm told, instead, I *am* out of water, and if I want to find water again, I must go in search of a different kind of water. *All* of us have been washed on the shore. We all have issues, we are all broken.

The brokenness we experience, the brokenness that mingles in our DNA, is a kind of fallout from the fall of man. Men and women were made to be in relationship with God, but because of the fall of man, we aren't.

The Scripture that states if an earthly father knows how to provide for his children, how much more God knows how to provide for his speaks volumes in its antithesis, too: if an earthly father abandons his children and wrecks their lives, how much more would an abandonment from God destroy a human being? As I look at humanity, I can only describe the human personality as designed for a relationship with something from which it has been separated. I hear it in conversations, read it in books, listen to it in music, interpret it through psychology, and so on and so on. The idea of this separation has come to feel obvious to me.

But this leaves us in a quandary, doesn't it? Some of you were abandoned by your fathers. And to come to you and say it wasn't only your father, but God too, would be unkind. The only bright side, if it could be considered bright, is that we are not alone. A hundred thousand fish flop alongside us.

But there is a difference between our human fathers and God. God did not leave because he wanted to; he left because he had to. His nature defines good, and people wanted something he didn't want. He separated himself from us, but he didn't abandon us.

I saw a movie recently about a soldier in a war, receiving the occasional letter from home, a picture of his son, a description from his wife. This is an example of separation without abandonment.

NOT LONG AGO, I went out to John's place and had breakfast. Terri makes a famous Saturday morning breakfast, and it all reminded me of the first weekend I stayed in the house. We ate, and I caught up with the kids, and then John said we should meet up in the apartment. Since I'd left, the space had been set up for Terri's parents, who visit often. They fixed up my old apartment as their permanent guest space.

"It's a lot cleaner now than when you lived here, Don," John said as we rounded the top step. He was right. Terri's mother's furniture was an improvement from my ratty couch and old chair. As I walked around, I remembered the piles of clothes and recalled the days when Chris tromped up the stairs to wake me in the morning. I went into the kitchen and could see in my mind the stacks of dishes in the sink, the boxes that I stacked in the hallway, too lazy to walk them down to the garage for storage.

"It even smells nice," I said.

"We had to hire a crew after you moved out. It took a few months of work, but we got the smell out," John said with a smile.

"Hey, I've changed," I defended.

"I know you have. I know you have," John said.

"You know, John, I remember you coming up one day and saying I would change. You looked around at the piles of clothes and said there would come a day when I couldn't live like that anymore. You were right."

"I know. Everybody grows up, Don."

When John and I settled in to talk, I went straight to it: My feeling that God doesn't want much to do with us—especially with me—I said the idea still tripped me up at times. I struggled to find the right words. "Maybe the feeling is more that he doesn't care, like he is busy with other people. Essentially, I didn't see God much different than I saw my friends' fathers when I was a kid. They were nice guys, you know, very kind and would love to help out, but I didn't belong to them. I was charity." Even as I said this, it felt true. It would be hard for John to convince me otherwise. "You know," John said, "we've talked about how a father, that is, a biological father, is a metaphor for God, and if the metaphor screws up, it's the metaphor's fault, not

God's. Let me ask you this, Don. Do you believe God is fathering you?"

"I think I do. I mean, looking back on my life, I see him giving me what I needed rather than what I wanted. And I know that to the degree I've stuck with him, sort of given him the benefit of the doubt, he's blessed my life."

"The reason God is fathering you," John said, "the reason he does what he does is because he has *not* abandoned you. The Scriptures use the word *Hesed*, which is a Greek word we don't have a good translation for. Essentially, it means *loyal love*. And loyal love doesn't abandon.

"I understand that you felt like a burden to your biological father. But you have to know, Don, God isn't burdened by you. He isn't frustrated with you, any more than I am frustrated with Chris, Elle, or Cassy."

"Right. And I know that. I know that intellectually," I told him.

"The thing about you and me," John continued, "is we can believe things that aren't true; I mean we can believe them deep in our bones. So I think the first thing you have to do is trust that when God says he loves to hear you talk to him, he really does. You have to tell yourself, as many times as it takes, that he loves you and isn't burdened by you."

"Right," I said, nodding my head and wondering how freeing it would be to believe that.

"You know, Chris is getting older now," John began, folding his hands, "and he's not talking to me as much as he used to. I mean we talk, but he confides in his friends more than he confides in me. So now, when Chris comes to me and confides in me, it means the world. He has my undivided attention. I delight in it, you know. So in a way, it's easier for me to believe that when God says he delights in me he really does, because I understand how that feels."

"So I need to be a father to understand."

"Well, it helps. And probably someday you will be. That's a stage of life. But also, you have to know, that as humans—as fallen creatures—we don't completely understand God. He is not like us, he is not fallen, he is pure love. God is at a disadvantage when he says he loves us, because the love we know is so broken. Think about it, Don. Love is conditional for everybody. It's a cheap version of the love God gives."

"And I believe that, like I said, but . . ."

"This is where faith comes in," he persisted. "Faith goes beyond the emotional. If you rely on your emotions, on how you feel, you are going to ride a roller coaster. As people who have faith in God, we can't let emotions dictate. We have to trust that what God says is true."

"So you just tell yourself to believe?" I questioned.

"Yes, that is what I do. And I'm not alone. Think about the Psalms of David, Psalm 103 and 112, Psalm 145, David wonders out loud where God is, often accusing him of abandoning him, and then he meditates and rehearses the truth, he commands his soul to believe the truth, and he returns to faith."

"That helps," I said. "That you can just act on something, even if you don't feel like you believe."

"Yeah, you can't have a good relationship with somebody if you don't trust they are on your side. Scripture says God is for us, and we have to believe it."

"But even more than that. We *obey* God. Scripture says if we love God, we will obey him. It's cause and effect. Most people turn it around and think of it like a dysfunctional father-and-son-relationship. We obey because we don't want to get in trouble. We obey because we want Dad's approval. We try to make obedience the cause and love the effect, but it doesn't work. We will eventually bag the whole thing. Love comes first."

"So, we have to feel love, then we will obey."

"You don't have to feel love, no," John disagreed. "You're assuming that love is a feeling. It isn't. It can involve feelings, but often it doesn't. Love acts out of faith, which rarely involves feelings. Love is action; it's deciding something is true and living out of that belief."

———————

JOHN AND I wrapped up our conversation that evening, and I said good-bye to Terri and the kids and to Papa Mac. As I walked to the car, I looked around the place, out at Mount Hood, up at my old bedroom window. It's true I didn't feel like the same person I was when I lived there. Everything John had said God would do, he did. He was bringing me into maturity. And on the long drive home, I kept thinking about the fact God had never abandoned me.

But I kept wondering about that initial question: How could God could allow such difficult things to happen? You and I know the wound of growing up without a father, but I'm talking about all the other wounds, all the other hardships human beings face, many of them so much more painful than ours.

I understood and even believed that the pain we experienced in the world wasn't God's fault. Mankind had chosen its own way, and God, because he is good, could not follow. But what were we supposed to do with the pain? We were just supposed to sit and be bitter?

An answer to that question came a little later through a book I had been reading called *Country of My Skull* by Antjie Krog. The book is about the Truth and Reconciliation Commission in South Africa. The TRC was a commission established by Nelson Mandela to listen to and attempt to reconcile the country after the atrocities of apartheid. But before the commission was established, government officials asked Bishop Desmond Tutu what sort of person should be considered for a position on the commission, and Tutu responded that the commission should be comprised of victims, of people whose lives had been ripped open by the horrors of oppression. But not arrogant victims, he stated, not people looking for vengeance. Instead, Tutu said softly, these should be people who have the authority of awful experiences, experiences that educated them toward empathy, and yet have within themselves hearts willing to forgive. This, he went on to clarify, could only be accomplished through a deeply buttressed spiritual life. These people would be *wounded healers*.

I knew as I read this that if these people who had suffered unconscionable wrongs could rise in dignity, God would expect nothing less from you and me, having encountered lesser pain. And I think Bishop Tutu's insight is a fitting thought with which to close this book. If I have a prayer for you and for the millions who were abandoned by fathers, it is that we would not be arrogant victims, but wounded healers. I can only perceive this as a dignified calling.

Acknowledgments

O riginally, this book was released as a co-written book. John MacMurray's help in the editing process was so substantial that I included his name on the first edition. As we took the book to a larger house, we made the decision to list a single author, which aids sales and clarifies the voice. But it goes without saying that John has allowed me to lay his life out in this book, and I am so grateful.

John, thank you for the great pleasure of your friendship. Sitting and talking with you, knowing you had better things to do with your time, I can only accept as a gift of grace. I can't repay you, but I will pass the kindness on to somebody else, which I suspect is all you want. Also special thanks to Terri, Chris, Elle, and Cassy MacMurray, who let me live in their home, and who accepted me as a member of their family. God is good, and you are all the evidence we need.

It is hard to imagine a person doing a better job of expressing love in the face of difficulty more than my mother. I didn't write much about Mom in this book, because she is a book of her own. After my sister and I left home, my mother, in her fifties, enrolled in night school and earned both her bachelor's and master's degrees. Mom, you are one of the greatest role models a person could have, and I am deeply grateful.

Special thanks to David Gentiles, Tara Brown, Jordan Green, David Allen, Jim Chaffee, Kathy Helmers, Rick McKinley, Kurt and Donna Nelson, Kaitie Nelson, Randy Alcorn, Jeff Foxworthy, Ernie Johnson, Tim Cash, Leonard and Elizabeth Sweet, Blake Gaskill, and Grant Gaskill for your help and encouragement. And to Dan, Matt, Charlie, and Stephen for letting me come on the road and read portions of the book to your great audiences. Nobody should receive that kind of honor. And thanks to John Eldredge, whose Wild at Heart Boot Camp provided a healing experience necessary for diving further into these issues.

Thanks to you for reading this book. It means the world, and I am grateful. Without you, I'd have to get a real job, driving busses or ferry boats, and that would put people in danger.

Reading Group Guide

This reading group guide for **Father Fiction** *includes an introduction, discussion questions, ideas for enhancing your book club, and a Q&A with author* **Donald Miller**. *The suggested questions are intended to help your reading group find new and interesting angles and topics for your discussion. We hope that these ideas will enrich your conversation and increase your enjoyment of the book.*

Introduction

Donald Miller grew up fatherless. As a young adult he was taken in by an intact family and discovered what he was missing by not having had a family. But even a fatherless child has a God interested in parenting him. With each essay, Donald explores the gaps that being fatherless left in him and how his readers can begin to fill these holes in their own lives.

Discussion Questions

1. Don's advice addresses gaps in his own development that came from not having a father in his life. Think about your father or fatherless experience. How did it impact your development?

2. Who were the mentors in your life? What contributions did they make in shaping you into the person you are today?

3. One of the themes in Don's book is that fatherless children grow up having a sense that they are a burden. How do you think that belief affects a child's development?

4. How does the notion of God fathering you strike you? As you imagine being parented by God, what kind of a parent do you imagine him to be?

5. Don wrote that mediating on the Lord's Prayer and understanding that God was parenting him led him to have a more hopeful view of the world. What are the possibilities that being parented by God opens up for you?

6. Don has a minimalistic view of manhood: "A man is an adult with a penis." Do you agree with Don or do you

believe that there are larger gender roles that define masculinity?

7. Don struggled to accept male authority in his life. Who are the people you allow to tell you the truth and give you correction?

8. Learning how to play chess reminded Don that life wasn't random and that he needed to approach it with patience and strategy. What disciplines have you built into your life to help you meet your goals?

9. In his chapter on dating, Don writes, "We are not going to get the love we really need from each other. We are going to get it from God, in heaven. Until then, we have an awesome opportunity to *practice* God's love with each other." If Don is right, how should that influence our expectations regarding romantic love?

10. Don wrote, "Men fantasize that sex is mere biology." Do you agree with that statement? If so, why do you think men fantasize this way? What are the consequences of this?

11. John taught Don to view work as worship. What does that phrase mean to you? Does work usually feel more like a curse, or more like worship?

12. Do you agree that complaining is a form of self-pity?

Why or why not? How can self-pity rob you of gaining emotional muscle?

13. "When you forgive, you bear the burden somebody has given you without holding them accountable." Have you ever had to navigate this type of forgiveness in your own life? What were the challenges?

14. The book closes with these words: "If I have a prayer for you and for the millions who were abandoned by fathers, it is that we would not be arrogant victims, but wounded healers." What would our society look like if it were filled with millions of these wounded healers?

Enhance Your Book Club

1. Visit www.census.gov and explore the extent of the impact fatherlessness has on your community. How big a problem is fatherlessness in your community? Invite a social worker whom one of your members knows to sit in on your next meeting and describe how he or she works to combat the effects of fatherlessness.

2. Think about the mentors who have shaped your life. Give one of them a phone call or write one of them a

letter to say thank you. It will mean the world to one of them.

3. Donald Miller responded to the crisis of American father-lessness by founding thementoringproject.org. Visit the website and look around. What response can you add?

4. Think of the wisdom that you've collected through your own learning and experiences. What types of wisdom could you pass on to someone else? Is there someone in your life whom you think you could mentor?

Author Q&A

Early in the book, you mention a collection of mentors who influenced you. How would your life be different if these men hadn't invested in you?

It's a bit hard to say. I think I would be cynical and bitter, and less mature, for sure. My main mentor, David Gentiles, taught me to love, to side with love, to be forgiving and gracious. I am not great at it now, but I know I would be terrible without his influence. I also think I wouldn't be very spiritual, I wouldn't think as much about God, and that makes me sad. My mentors showed me that spirituality and masculinity go hand in hand. I owe a great deal to these guys.

What did you discover about yourself as you wrote this book? What have you had to unlearn from the experience of growing up without a father?

No book I've written has changed me as much as this book. It was a healing experience, for sure. I learned I had issues from growing up without a father, and this book put me on a path toward healing. I am grateful, personally, for the experience. I would say I am stronger for having written this book, more tender, less filled with self-pity and more confident.

You quote President Eisenhower, who said his parents believed "the world could be fixed of its problems if every child understood the necessity of their existence." If mentoring became a prominent theme in our culture, what problems would be solved?

I don't think they would be solved, no. But I think our culture would be significantly different. I think we'd have fewer people in prison, and women would be happier because men would have better character. To say that a mentor can replace a dad is to say too much. But a mentor can change a child's life, for sure.

The act of writing this book provoked a personal response from you. Tell us about The Mentoring Project.

As I was working on the book, I realized the issue needed more than a book, that kids needed positive male role models. We have a serious masculinity crisis in this country for lack of positive male role models. And having grown up in the church, I realized we had all these churches embedded in communities across the country and I realized the infrastructure was there to reach out to all these kids. There are 27 million kids growing up without fathers and 360,000 churches, so the church is poised to help on this issue more than any other institution. So we started a little mentoring program in Portland, at my local church, and that spread to another and another and another. Now we are mentoring lots of kids in Portland and looking to branch out across the country.

How has serving on President Obama's National Fatherhood Initiative shaped how you view the crisis of American fatherlessness?

At first it was disheartening, because I realized the problem was enormous, but the more we talked, the more we realized the issue could be confronted in a realistic and effective way by the church. I think it could be one of the most powerful initiatives the church has embraced, to mentor fatherless boys and shut down prisons. I also realized that the government didn't have a lot of solutions. They are doing a remarkable job helping single moms, but they are unable to provide positive male role models, which is the root of the problem. We can do that through the church.

Don, you have pretty minimalistic definition of what a man is (a person with a penis). Why do you think there's

a whole industry of books and media aimed at helping males understand manhood if it's so simple?

Well, I actually don't think it's that simple. Many of those books are good, and I encourage young men to read them, but it's true that when I read them as a kid I felt left out. I was trying to encourage the young men who feel left out, who doubt their masculinity. But manhood is complicated. I do believe a person with a penis is male, and there's no refuting it, but to be a good man, we have to work on ourselves and become men of good character. That takes effort and wisdom, so those books are appropriate.

What are some of the best examples of mentoring that you've observed in our culture?

I think youth pastors are our best mentors. They are great. They are some of the most important people in our culture, and I love them. They can be treated like second-class citizens in churches, or just passers-through on the way to a more prominent position in a church, but there's no question they are affecting the future of our country. Teachers are also influential, but youth pastors can engage the heart in the way a teacher is limited, and real healing comes when you embrace the heart.

You said in an interview that it will be a long time before you write another memoir. So what new direction do you see your creativity taking?

I'm writing a book about story, now, about how to shape your life like a story. It's a follow-up to *A Million Miles in a Thousand Years*. I am not sure what will come after that. Perhaps a more creative project, or even a book of poems. Something more literary. But I want to get this story message out first. I love talking about it and thinking about it.

About the Author

Donald Miller is the founder of The Mentoring Project, a non-profit equipping churches to mentor the fatherless generation. He serves on the Presidential Task Force on Fatherhood and Healthy Families. He is the author of numerous books, and lives in Portland, Oregon.

For more information about Donald Miller, please visit: www.donmilleris.com.

THE MENTORING PROJECT
www.thementoringproject.org

After growing up without a father and learning about
the American crisis of fatherlessness,
Donald Miller founded the Mentoring Project in 2008.

The Mentoring Project seeks to respond to
the American crisis of fatherlessness
by inspiring and equipping faith communities
to mentor fatherless boys.

Your generous donation of $10 per month
will provide a life-changing mentor to a fatherless boy and
rewrite the story of the fatherless generation.

Please visit www.thementoringproject.org to donate
and learn more.

*I believe in the power of story and invite you into the new
story we are telling. I believe we can rewrite the story of
the fatherless generation. This narrative does not have to
be cyclical. It can end with fewer men in prison, less families abandoned, and the fatherless being cared for by positive role models who believe, like I do, that we can choose
to live a better story.*

—Donald Miller